Globalisation

FOR THE COMMON GOOD

Also by Kamran Mofid

DEVELOPMENT PLANNING IN IRAN: FROM MONARCHY
TO ISLAMIC REPUBLIC

THE ECONOMIC CONSEQUENCES OF THE GULF WAR

Globalisation

FOR THE COMMON GOOD

KAMRAN MOFID

SHEPHEARD-WALWYN (PUBLISHERS) LTD

© Kamran Mofid 2002

All rights reserved. No part of this book may be
reproduced in any form without the written permission
of the publisher, Shepheard-Walwyn (Publishers) Ltd

First published in 2002 by
Shepheard-Walwyn (Publishers) Ltd
Suite 604, The Chandlery
50 Westminster Bridge Road
London SE1 7QY

British Library Cataloguing in Publication Data
A catalogue record of this book
is available from the British Library

ISBN 0 85683 195 6

Typeset by Alacrity
Banwell Castle, Weston-super-Mare
Printed by St Edmundsbury Press, Bury St Edmunds

Few can contemplate without a sense of exhilaration the splendid achievements of practical energy and technical skill, which, from the latter part of the seventeenth century, were transforming the face of material civilisation, and of which England was the daring, if not too scrupulous, pioneer. If, however, economic ambitions are good servants, they are bad masters.

The most obvious facts are the most easily forgotten. Both the existing economic order and too many of the projects advanced for reconstructing it break down through their neglect of the truism that, since even quite common men have souls, no increase in material wealth will compensate them for arrangements which insult their self-respect and impair their freedom. A reasonable estimate of economic organisation must allow for the fact that, unless industry is to be paralysed by recurrent revolts on the part of outraged human nature, it must satisfy criteria which are not purely economic.

R.H. TAWNEY[1]

The truth that I have tried to make clear will not find easy acceptance. If that could be, it would have been accepted long ago. If that could be, it would never have been obscured. But it will find friends – those who will toil for it; suffer for it; if need be, die for it. This is the power of Truth.

HENRY GEORGE[2]

To the memory of my friend and mentor
George Bull, OBE, FRSL,
(23rd August, 1929 – 6th April, 2001)
for what I am and what I do

Make me an instrument of your peace,
Where there is hatred, let me sow love,
Where there is injury, pardon,
Where there is doubt, faith,
Where there is despair, hope,
Where there is darkness, light,
And where there is sadness, joy.

O Master, grant that I may not seek,
so much to be consoled as to console,
To be understood as to understand,
To be loved as to love.

For it is in giving that we receive,
It is in pardoning that we are pardoned,
And it is in dying that we are born to eternal life.

THE PRAYER OF ST FRANCIS OF ASSISI

Contents

Acknowledgements

IN PREPARING THIS PROJECT, I have benefited greatly from discussions and deliberations with many interested scholars and thinkers. I have also received much support from different corners. I am grateful to the students at Plater College (2000-2001) for sharing the gifts of love, hope, faith and learning with me. At times, in the process of life, one can be found guilty of arrogance: they taught me again the beauty of humbleness. Of course the same could be said about all the students that I have been honoured and privileged to teach in the last twenty-five years or so. They all have been a great source of inspiration. Furthermore, I am grateful for the teachings, discussions, deliberations, friendship and support of others at Plater. In particular I am most grateful to Michael Blades, the Principal. Without his support, care and friendship, it would not have been possible to pursue and develop this project. I am also thankful to Sr Collette, Greg Glazov, Pat Edge, Barry Hudd, Emma Schackle, Stratford Caldecott and Fr Noel Mullin. I am richer for knowing them.

I am in particular indebted to my late friend and mentor, George Bull, to whom this study is dedicated. We undertook many scholarly works together. However, above all, he taught me much about what is good in Catholicism, its deep and constant respect for justice, equality, love, solidarity and the common good, as well as the Church's love and care for the disadvantaged, marginalized and excluded. I learned from him about true Catholicism and its respect for others, its ecumenism, and inter-faith dialogue. He introduced me to Vatican Council II, especially the document *Nostra Aetate*. For all his fatherly love to me, I am eternally grateful.

I am also grateful to Professors James Piscatori and Brian Ray of the Oxford Centre for Islamic Studies, and Newman College, Birmingham, respectively, for their continuous friendship, support and inspiration.

I should also like to thank Monsignor Canon Thomas Gavin of St Thomas More, Coventry, for his constant friendship, support and care during the last twenty-five years. I am also grateful to my Catenian Association Brothers at Kenilworth Circle for their comradeship, solidarity and friendship.

My thanks are also due to Canon Paul Oestreicher, former Director of the International Centre for Reconciliation at Coventry Cathedral and the Very Reverend John Petty, Dean Emeritus of Coventry Cathedral, for their love, friendship and support. Through them I learned the beauty and significance of dialogue and reconciliation. With their support and encouragement I was able to co-found, with George Bull, a centre for the study of forgiveness and reconciliation at Coventry.

I am also grateful to my editor, Anthony Werner at Shepheard-Walwyn for his moral, spiritual and academic support. Without Anthony's input, publishing this book would have been a much more difficult and daunting experience. Likewise, I extend very warm appreciation to Jean Desebrock for her excellent work and personal support on the production of the book. I am also grateful to Alan Downs for the book's jacket artwork and illustration.

Last and most of all, I owe an enormous debt to my wife Annie and my sons Kevin and Paul. I owe particular thanks to Annie, who more than anyone else has discussed the issues raised in this study with me over the years. For the content and style of this book as well as my previous works I owe much to her. Without my wife and my sons there would have been no dreams to fulfil.

Finally, any failure to comprehend is due completely to my own shortcomings.

Abstract

TODAY THE GLOBALISED WORLD ECONOMY, despite many significant achievements during the last few decades, and especially since the end of the Second World War, in areas such as science, technology, medicine, transportation and communication, is facing major catastrophic socio-economic, political, cultural and environmental crises.

We are surrounded by global problems of inequality, injustice, poverty, greed, marginalisation, exclusion, intolerance, fear, mistrust, xenophobia, terrorism, sleaze and corruption. These problems are affecting the overall fabric of societies in many parts of the world.

In 1944, at a UN Conference in Bretton Woods, the World Bank, the International Monetary Fund (IMF) and a global free-trade agenda were launched. According to the then United States Treasurey Secretary, this was to stimulate 'the creation of a dynamic world economy'. Given what has happened since, it seems that a prime purpose was to ensure American corporations increased access to new markets and raw materials.

More recently, the World Trade Organisation (WTO) was established in 1995 to continue the corporate agenda. The former Director-General of the WTO described it as 'a constitution for a single global economy', while the *Economist* called it an 'embryo world government'. Once again, however, given what has happened since, it appears that the real purpose of the WTO has been to engineer the elimination of all barriers to trade, for the benefit of the strongest. In effect, it is becoming illegal for elected governments around the world to hinder the profits of big corporations. An 'embryo world government' ... and yet no one voted for it. Pertinent questions at this point are: To whom is the WTO accountable? Where is the manifesto for their policies? Which citizens of the world campaigned and voted for them?

Globalisation has led to radical changes in the way we live. The goals that were set over fifty years ago remain unchanged and, in fact, have been achieved many times over. Since the conference in 1944 at Bretton Woods, the world has witnessed a twelve-fold increase in global trade and a five-fold increase in economic growth. However, during the same period, the world in every aspect has significantly deteriorated. Today, at the dawn of the third millennium, over three billion people survive on less than $2 a day. Per capita income continues to fall in 80 countries, while life expectancy has declined in 33 countries since the early 1990s. It has been observed that 24,000 people worldwide, 75% of them children under five, die every day from starvation or malnutrition, for want of basic food in this supposedly globalised world of plenty. Moreover, 7,000 people, mainly in Africa, die every day from Aids for want of drugs that are available in the West.

Meanwhile, the global environment lies close to catastrophic destruction, with major life-threatening consequences for all of us, rich as well as poor. In all, in this globalisation a handful of big corporations are ruling us, controlling our minds as well as our bodies. Globalisation for them means giving big business access to a global market, to produce as cheaply as possible, and to make huge profits for their shareholders, with no regard for the rest of us. In their greed they show no loyalty to place or citizens. They come and go as they please. What happens to a society or community as a result of their actions is of no interest to them.

It is my firm belief that economics, and the way in which it has been taught at our universities worldwide, bears a major responsibility for the existence and persistence of these crises. Modern economics has major shortcomings: it concentrates almost totally on self-interest motives and shows little respect for, or understanding of, the true human values of community, solidarity, common good, morality, ethics and justice. Moreover, in the words of Pope John Paul II, Western culture is marked by 'the fatal attempt to secure the good of humanity by eliminating God'.

Finally, I believe that, since the recent 'appointment' of the new American President, the task of this book has become

more urgent and more vital. The new American administration wasted no time in perverting international bodies into
tools for the advancement of American business interests,
assisting them further to Americanise the world in the name
of globalisation. This President, more than any other, has been
supported by the corporate sector. His administration firmly
and unashamedly believes that everything should be subordinate to neo-classical economics. Their policies on global
warming, arms control, the UN, world trade and the international criminal court – to mention but a few from a long
list – do not suggest an administration committed to build-
ing an ethical, moral and just world order.

There could scarcely be a more timely, indeed urgent,
moment for a fresh examination of what has become known
as 'globalisation'.

CHAPTER 1

✳

Many feel completely lost. Only a few still dare to be critical and ask what the reasons are for the present threat to the lives of human beings and to nature, and whether there are any alternatives.

ULRICH DUCHROW[1]

You might not see things yet on the surface, but underground, it's already on fire.

Y.B. MANGUNWIJAYA[2]

Capitalism is an affront to the equal valuation of human beings and a denial of human freedom. It is a system of structural inequality and unfreedom, wrapped around with layers of ideological mystification.

R.H. TAWNEY[4]

CHAPTER 1

Introduction

IN THE LAST FEW DECADES, and especially since the end of the Second World War, there have been massive achievements in the growth of industrialisation and modernisation. Without much difficulty, we can see all around us evidence of quantum leaps in the development of science, medicine, information technology, transportation, communication, finance, banking, and much else. Today the pace of change is breathtaking. According to Hutton and Giddens, it is the interaction of extraordinary technological innovation with worldwide reach, driven by a global capitalism, that gives today's change its particular complexities and complexion. 'It has now a speed, inevitability and force that it has not had before.'³ Following the collapse of Communism with its planned economy, the transmission system for all changes taking place today is market capitalism – now unchallenged as the means through which the world organises its economy and society.

Considering the achievements, the pace of change and globalisation, one with a charitable inclination towards my profession could argue that economics and economists have made a major positive contribution to the world. However, given the extent and persistence of so many catastrophic crises at local, national and global levels, I and many others can equally argue that there are major shortcomings within the discipline of economics. These shortcomings need to be identified, analysed and debated: otherwise, in my view, the crises will become so out of hand that the fundamentals of human existence and our shared civilisation could be seriously undermined.

This, in a nutshell, is the concern of this book. I hope to

3

identify some of the crises and the reasons for them, and to debate and analyse them, in order to provide constructive alternatives to current destructive ideas and models. I hope the book will prove to be a journey from wasteland to promised land. In developing these thoughts, I am influenced by the statements of three scholars who share my concerns. These are quoted at the beginning of this chapter.

What are the main crises faced by modern societies? There are global problems of inequality, injustice, poverty, marginalisation and exclusion. There is also the crisis of environmental degradation and global warming. Furthermore, there is a huge rise in crime, corruption and sleaze. While globalisation and revolutionary improvements in communication and transportation have brought many of us closer together, they have also resulted in a mass migration from the poorer South to the richer North. Xenophobia, fear, mistrust and intolerance are affecting the overall fabric of societies in many parts of the world and are an ongoing problem.

Despite advances in material well-being we have not become happier in the process. Most of us have maximised our profits and incomes but we are not at ease with ourselves and with others. What seems to have happened is that we have all become producers and consumers with no generally agreed set of assumptions on theological, moral, ethical and spiritual values – a point to which I shall return later.

To expand the above observation, the following was noted by George Bull[5] and is most revealing. Pause for thought:

In 1923, a very important meeting was held at Edgewater Beach Hotel in Chicago. Attending this meeting were nine of the world's most 'successful' financiers. Those present were: the President of the largest independent steel company; the President of the largest utility company; the President of the largest gas company; the greatest wheat speculator; the President of the New York stock exchange; a member of the President's cabinet; the greatest 'bear' in Wall Street; the head of the world's greatest monopoly; and the President of the Bank of International Settlement. This, we must admit, was a gathering of some of the world's most successful men – or at least men who had found the secret of making money.

Twenty-five years later (in 1948) let us see what had happened to these men: the President of the largest independent steel company had died, bankrupt, having lived on borrowed money for five years before his death; the President of the largest utility company had died a fugitive from justice, penniless in a foreign land; the President of the largest gas company was insane; the greatest wheat speculator had died abroad – insolvent; the President of the New York stock exchange had recently been released from Sing Sing penitentiary; the member of the President's cabinet had been pardoned from prison so that he could die at home; the greatest 'bear' in Wall Street had died – a suicide; the head of the world's greatest monopoly had died – a suicide; the President of the Bank of International Settlement had died – a suicide.

'All these men learned well the art of making money, but not one of them learned how to live,' commented the compiler of this list. Although, as George Bull admits, the list is surely wickedly contrived and selective, nonetheless it is a good reminder of the importance of moral and ethical perspectives in international business. Today, as in 1923, after many global achievements, we have still in most cases succeeded materially at the expense of spiritual development and enrichment. Indeed there have been huge increases in the numbers of cases of loneliness, isolation, homelessness, stress, anxiety, depression, racism, intolerance, alcoholism, drug abuse, child neglect, divorce, suicide, and other evils.

In the process of modernisation and industrialisation we have become more and more individualistic, more secular. We have lost the art of empathy and sympathy. Progress has been at the expense of comradeship, solidarity, concern for others and a sense of the common good.

We must now ask the questions 'What has gone wrong?' and 'What can be done about it?'

I should like to answer the second question first. The solution lies in the reintroduction of faith, morality and ethics into our lives, personal as well as economic. In my view, religion can play a pivotal role in reversing the current trends.

To answer the question 'What has gone wrong?' I shall

argue, in the light of my own experience as a lecturer in economics for over twenty years, that the way the subject is taught all over the world is the central reason for our current failings. There has been too great an emphasis on self-interest, narrowly interpreted, as the sole motivator of economic action; an excessive reliance on mathematics and IT, and on almost incomprehensible jargon; an aversion to co-operation with other disciplines in the humanities and social sciences in order to carry out joint research and formulate broad-based policies; and above all an inability or unwillingness to address economic issues in the context of ethics, morality and faith.

After all, many of the issues that people fight over, or their governments put forward, have ultimately economics at their core – issues such as jobs, wages, income, profits, investment, growth, taxes, interest rates, production, consumption and trade.[6]

We, the economists, have habitually blamed others for society's failures. 'If only they had listened to us ...', we argue when things go wrong. I should like to put the record straight. I want, in this study, to be inward-looking and self-examining. I want to depart from the textbooks and allow wisdom to prevail.

In order to provide alternatives, I shall argue that the teaching of economics in our high schools and universities should become more down to earth, more in touch with reality, more in line with our human needs and language. We have had enough of incomprehensible jargon and complicated mathematics. Economics should give more thought to the human dimensions of religion, faith, morality and ethics.[7]

At this point I must stress that under no circumstances am I against economics, market economy, earning the fruits of risk-taking, globalisation, production or consumption *per se*. What I am against is the concentration on self-interest at the expense of all other dimensions in economic decision-making. In the words of Paul Ormerod, writing in *The Death of Economics*, 'Innovation, entrepreneurship and profits are still essential. Economic competition exists on a global scale, and economies must be equipped for it. But economic success can be achieved, and achieved more successfully, within a broader and more beneficial framework than that driven by the pure, individual rationality of the economics text books.'[8]

Economics needs to return to its original roots. Let us not forget that Adam Smith, author of *An Inquiry into the Nature and Causes of the Wealth of Nations*, 'father of modern economics' and 'mentor' to many economists and politicians, was first and foremost a Professor of Moral Philosophy at the University of Glasgow and, before he wrote *Wealth of Nations*, was already famous for his great work, *The Theory of Moral Sentiments*[9] – more of this in future chapters. Economics and the economy could be better understood and appreciated in this context.

Given the above, the words of John Young ring true: 'a true grasp of how the economy should be constituted shows it to be a thing of harmony and beauty, all its parts co-operating for the common good, and its inbuilt laws distributing benefits equitably.'[10] In short, the focus of economics should be on the benefits and the bounty that the economy produces, on how to let this bounty increase, and how to share the benefits justly among the people, to the common good, removing the evils that hinder this process.[11]

A further point is that, in attempting to industrialise and modernise, our main objective, it seems, has been to increase our material and financial well-being regardless of the true cost. In the process, through the main teachings of economics and the workings of the economic world, we have become individualistic and self-centred. In the words of Pope John Paul II, in his message on World Peace Day, 1st January 2001, 'Western cultural models are alluring because of their remarkable scientific and technical qualities, yet, there is growing evidence of their deepening human, spiritual and moral impoverishment.' The Pope then observes that, 'Western culture is marked by the fatal attempt to secure the good of humanity by eliminating God.'

In the light of the above statement, which I strongly endorse, I offer the following, which is based on personal as well as academic experience.

When I was growing up, I was much encouraged to believe in one God, the ultimate reality, the unconditioned one, the

Holy God, the maker of Heaven and Earth, of all that is seen and unseen. I was encouraged to love him and to worship him in spirit and truth. I was encouraged to trust him, to praise him and to pray to him. Above all, I was guided to act ethically and be good to, and do good for, others. Today, the globalised capitalist economy has emptied our churches and other places of worship; it has catastrophically weakened the ethical and moral dimensions of our societies.

Today, in place of the one God that I was encouraged to believe in, we have been offered many global gods to worship. For many people, today's gods include the likes of Nike, Adidas, Levi, Calvin Klein, American Express, Nokia, AOL, Microsoft, Disneyland, Coca-Cola, McDonalds and Carling Black Label.[12]

Following the destruction of Sunday as we knew it, there has been a drastic decline in church attendance. Today's global churches are the shopping malls, the superstores and factory outlets, many of them open twenty-four hours a day for maximum worship! Madeleine Bunting's contribution to the 'Common Good' debate in *The Guardian* (21st March 2001) is most telling:

... Christianity may have steeply declined but its language still permeates the public sector – words such as 'service' and 'vocation'. A belief in altruistic, self-sacrificing service was a central thread running through the lives of many public servants and inspired great respect amongst those who encountered it. But from the 1960s onwards, secularisation introduced a new concept of duty to oneself along with a language of personal emotional needs and fulfilment which has powerfully reorientated the individual towards a preoccupation with self. Personal identity has been severed from any wider collective context such as class, creed or nationality. The decline of these collective identities of nation, faith and ideology – has left a vacuum and has been taken over and exploited by consumer culture. The most powerful collective identities now are those we buy: DKNY or CK mean more to your average teenager than any government service. Where once socialism offered the promise of a better world, now GAP does. Nike sells its flash on the heroic myth of near superhuman individual effort and achievement. Where once every seven-year-old girl wanted to be a teacher or a nurse, now they want to be Britney Spears. We have a culture of individual aggrandisement and self-promotion in which self-effacing service has no place ... But the government's voice is drowned out by consumer

culture which is primarily focused on your relationship with yourself rather
than a relationship with a wider collective: it is typified by the L'Oreal
slogan, 'Because you're worth it.' Brands are monikers to exclusivity, so
they exclude as many as they include. Besides, DKNY is belonging to
what? In that quest, a vision of the common good to which a new generation can subscribe is strikingly absent.[13]

To conclude my observations on the above topic, the following statement by Brian Griffiths is noteworthy: 'I believe
this is precisely what the "crisis of capitalism" is about. It is
nothing less than the crisis of humanism as a religion being
played out in economic life.' He goes on, 'If freedom is made
an absolute, as it is for example in the writings of Milton
Friedman and Friedrich Hayek, such that it is impossible on
intellectual grounds to place limits on the exercise of freedom,
the result is an economic system shorn of justice ... My con-
tention is that both the injustice and inhumanity of capitalist
societies result inevitably from the failure to assert certain
absolutes and so place proper limits on the use of freedom.'[14]

Although I defend certain positive benefits of a well controlled, regulated and accountable market economy, I also
maintain that there can be no civilised marketplace without
morality, ethics or religion. I will argue that the solution to
the current socio-economic global crises is not technical. It
needs to be looked at again in a fresh way that will embrace
human values of morality, ethics and faith. In my view, the reintroduction of religious values and principles of justice can
play a pivotal role in reversing the current trends. As Ulrich
Duchrow and his associates have observed, this coincides with
Jesus' vision of God's kingdom in which the leading perspective is not the profit of the fittest, as in neo-liberal globalisation, but the rescue and empowerment of the weakest.[15]

For true believers in Christ, the following questions, in
my view, are of the utmost importance:

If, according to Ephesians 1, God is preparing in human history that
everyone and everything is brought under the Lordship of Jesus Christ,
His Shepherd – King – His own globalisation, shouldn't then caring
and sharing for and with each other be the main characteristic of our
lifestyle, instead of giving in fully to the secular trend of a growing
consumerism? What has happened to the basic teaching of common

stewardship and Christian solidarity with the suffering neighbours who in fact are the members of the same body of Christ?'[16]

I should like to reaffirm my belief that religion – and in the context of this book, Christianity, Catholicism – offers a just perspective and provides ethical and moral solutions to problems of political economy and the workings of the marketplace. To this end this study will seek to find out in more detail what has gone wrong with economics. Given our concerns, we need to understand what economics used to be considered and what it is now. Chapter 2 will attempt to provide a working definition.

For me, the massive rise of indebtedness and poverty in the Third World, combined with poverty, marginalisation and the exclusion of the great majority in the First World, are clear signs of the failure of the capitalist world economy. To highlight this catastrophic failure, in Chapter 3 I shall attempt to provide an analysis of these issues.

Because I believe that religion offers a just and ethical perspective on today's capitalist globalised economy, in Chapter 4 I shall debate some aspects of the social teachings of the Catholic Church. Given the limitations of this study, I shall concentrate on the meaning and consequences of solidarity, subsidiarity and the common good.

Chapter 5 is where I shall complete my journey from wasteland to promised land. Alternative models to the current one will be suggested. Here theological and ethical arguments will embrace our economic mind and come up with practical proposals for a life-enhancing economy.

In this study, as already stated, in attempting to provide a theological and ethical alternative to the current capitalist world economy, my emphasis will be on Catholic social teachings. However, it is important to say that my arguments should be seen as inclusive rather than exclusive. I see myself more as a believer in, and follower of, inter-religious dialogue than as a missionary crusader. I am open to inclusivity rather than closed in exclusivity. I have a message that I want to share with as many people as possible: not only with Catholics but also with believers in the other great religions of mankind. In a personal letter to me from the Dalai Lama, he writes that 'all the major religions of the world have equal potential to transform people into good human beings ... each religious tradition is a great source of inspiration for the millions of their followers.'

I believe that by empowering others to share with me, I will empower myself to share with them; by empowering others to teach me, I will empower myself to teach them. In this way I can spread the 'Good News' of the 'Catholic Social Teachings' to a much wider audience than if I were exclusive.

In reaching this state of mind, I have more than anything been influenced by the writings and statements of Pope John Paul II. His great works on ecumenism and his dialogues with others have provided me with a major source of inspiration. I have also been guided by the tireless efforts of Cardinal Francis Arinze and Bishop Michael Fitzgerald, President and Secretary respectively of the Pontifical Council for Inter-religious Dialogue. The document *Nostra Aetate* (*In Our Times*), from Vatican Council II, has also been a great source of guidance and inspiration.[17]

In Chapter 6, I shall discuss the possibility of an inter-religious common front, and common hope, to address our global crises.

CHAPTER 2

✳

Systemic, universal brainwashing is the crime, tendentious mental conditioning calculated to mislead students, to impoverish their mental ability, to bend their minds to the service of a system that funnels power and wealth to a parasitic minority.

MASON GAFFNEY[1]

Good economists know, from work carried out within their discipline, that the foundations of their subject are virtually non-existent ... Conventional economics offers prescriptions for the problems of inflation and unemployment which are at best misleading and at worst dangerously wrong ... Despite its powerful influence on public life, its achievements are as limited as those of pre-Newtonian physics ... it is to argue that conventional economics offers a very misleading view of how the world actually operates, and it needs to be replaced.

PAUL ORMEROD[2]

An orderly society is not, by itself, sufficient to satisfy human needs. Tyrants have a knack for enforcing order, but they exact a price that many people would rather not pay. Most of us expect the rules that establish order to be synchronised with the principles of Justice ... Capitalism lacks that moral basis, for its emphasis on self-interest, and the rights of the individual, are not properly balanced by the collective rights of the community. Justice, therefore, was something that reformers had to graft onto the outer skin of the system, for it had not been built into the foundations.

FRED HARRISON[3]

One reason why this is extraordinary is that economics is supposed to be concerned with real people. It is hard to believe that real people could be completely unaffected by the reach of the self-examination induced by the Socratic

question, 'How should one live?' ... a central motivating
one for ethics. Can the people whom economics studies
really be so unaffected by this resilient question and stick
exclusively to the rudimentary hard-headedness attributed
to them by modern economics?

AMARTYA SEN[4]

Whether it be politics, philosophy, religion or anything else,
the one cardinal characteristic of truth is simplicity. The
greatest truths that man ever heard were spoken in the language of simplicity in the streets of Jerusalem. Simplicity
and truth stand together, and whenever you get complexity, beware, because there is a falsity somewhere.

ANDREW MacLAREN[5]

Modern society is sick through the absence of a moral ideal
... The essence of all morality is this: to believe that every
human being is of infinite importance, and therefore that
no consideration of expediency can justify the oppression of
one by another. But to believe this it is necessary to believe
in God ... It is only when we realise that each individual
soul is related to a power above other men, that we are able
to regard each as an end in itself.

R.H. TAWNEY[6]

CHAPTER 2

What Economics Was,
What Economics Is:
A Journey from Promised Land
to Wasteland

O N THE PREVIOUS PAGES, we heard the voices of a
select minority of scholars – mainly economists –
daring to question and criticise orthodox economics.
We heard their concerns about what it has become today, and
about the way the subject is being taught. We have also heard
their voices on the subject of the major shortcomings of
modern economics, with its near total concentration on individualism and self-interest, and its lack of respect for, and
understanding of, the true human values of community, solidarity, common good, morality, ethics and justice. These very
issues which have been glossed over by modern economics are
those in greatest need of closer examination. They are the gist
of this chapter, indeed of this whole book. Through my experience of lecturing economics over the past twenty years or so,
I have nothing but respect and admiration for the inspiring
works of Professors Sen, Gaffney and Ormerod.[7] To this distinguished list we can add the works of scholars such as
Duchrow, Coward, Maguire, Young, Harrison, Hudson,
Miller, Feder, Schumacher, Andelson, Dawsey, Susan George,
Henry George, Potter, Elfstrom, Alves, Niebuhr, Richards,
McOustra and Charles SJ.[8]

At this point I should like to emphasise that I have also
heard the voices of the majority, those who so bravely try to
make the shortcomings of economics known to the public at
large; those who question the ethics of globalisation, GM

15

foods, and the workings of capitalism in general. I have also heard the voice of Jubilee 2000: millions of Christians from thousands of Churches around the world have been involved in the campaign to achieve a substantial debt reduction for the poorest countries of the Third World.

I have heard the voices of campaigners against global capitalism in London, Birmingham, Seattle, Prague, Davos, Nice, Melbourne, Washington DC, Quebec, Genoa and elsewhere. These are mainly ordinary, concerned people of good will, all interested in the common good, social and corporate responsibility, the environment, community and solidarity. These people, like me, are not against globalisation *per se*. They are against elite globalisation and for grass-roots globalisation. The first, which is top-downwards globalisation, is characterised by a constant drive to maximise profits in order to satisfy the greed of globe-spanning corporations. The second centres on life values, on protecting human rights and the environment. In all, the great majority of these protesters are beginning a movement that puts the love of life, and respect for the environment and ecology, above the love of money, and greed.

If I can, in a very small and humble way, discuss some of these concerns further, and bring about a closer link between the 'minorities' and 'majorities', then this study will have achieved a great deal. Ultimately, 'the study of economics is only of any value if it enables the human lot to be improved'.[9]

In Chapter 1 some of the main shortcomings of economics were identified. I noted the concentration on self-interest in mainstream economics, and its lack of interaction with ethics, morality and religion. However, if we return to the origins of economics, beginning with Aristotle, and also consider Adam Smith, centuries later, we see that in their studies issues such as ethics and morality had a pivotal and central role.

Before I attempt to analyse their work, and compare it with what economics has become today, the following points should be noted. Given the scope and limitations of this study, it is not possible to provide a detailed analysis of ethics and morality, their origins and development, their different meanings and interpretations. From the dawn of man's creation this area of study has absorbed and concerned him; the subject has been embraced by humanists, secular philosophers and religious thinkers alike. Their writings are discussed most eloquently elsewhere.[10] For the purposes of this study, it is sufficient to ponder Daniel Maguire's words:

We have become newly aware of that delicate marvel that made a surprising appearance on the surface of the earth. It is precarious and fragile and weight-wise almost insignificant, since it is less than a billionth of the weight of the whole planet. Many things militate against its survival, and that concerns us, because the name we give to this phenomenon – perhaps the only manifestation of it in all the folds of the universe – is *life*.[11]

According to Maguire, it is the systematic effort to know and to enhance the values of life which is called ethics. The name we give to our response to the preciousness we find in life is religion – a preciousness so great that it elicits from us our supreme encomium, our ultimate superlative: 'sacred'. Religion, according to Maguire, is our response to the sacred. 'Ethics and religion are twinned. What enhances life and its milieu we call moral: its mysterious and awe-filled grandeur we call holy.'[12]

On this point, Maguire finally notes that the experience of life as good to the point of holy is the foundation of civilisation. Law and political and economic theory are liege to our experience of the sanctity of life, which experience has animated literature and given soul to our art. Those swirling, symbol-packed movements we call religious are our main source of the moral attitudes that become the basal assumptions of law, politics and economics.

Understanding this helps us in our study of what economics used to be and what it is today. Our starting point is with ethics, morality and religion.

Professor Amartya Sen, in his significant study *On Ethics and Economics*, demonstrates that, in its recent development, a serious distancing between economics and ethics has brought about one of the major deficiencies in contemporary economic theory. Sen argues that modern economics could become more productive by paying greater and more explicit attention to the ethical considerations that shape human behaviour and judgement. However, as he has so correctly observed, there is a surprising contrast between the self-consciously 'non-ethical' character of modern economics and its historical evolution as an offshoot of ethics.[13]

The ethics-related tradition of economics goes back at least as far as Aristotle. Robert Solomon[14] has argued that Aristotle deserves recognition as the first economist – two thousand years before Adam Smith. Aristotle distinguished between two different aspects of economics: *oikonomikos* or household trading, which he approved of and thought essential to the working of any even modestly complex society, and *chrematisike*, which is trade for profit. Aristotle declared the latter activity wholly devoid of virtue and called those who engaged in such purely selfish practices 'parasites'. His attack on the unsavoury and unproductive practice of 'usury', as identified by Solomon, held force virtually until the fifteenth century, when John Calvin's writings started greatly to influence the study of economics. The extension of Calvinism to all spheres of human activity was extremely important to a world emerging from an agrarian medieval economy into a commercial industrial era. Calvin accepted the newborn capitalism and encouraged trade and production, while, most importantly, opposing the abuses of exploitation and self-indulgence. Industrialisation was stimulated by the concepts of thrift, industry, sobriety, and responsibility that Calvin preached as essential to the achievement of the reign of God on earth.

However, in the eighteenth century, with the publication of Adam Smith's masterwork, *The Wealth of Nations*, there was a quantum leap in many aspects of economics. Now *chrematisike* became the driving force and primary virtue of modern society – a point to which I shall return later.

As Sen points out, at the very beginning of *The Nicomachean Ethics* Aristotle relates the subject of economics to human ends, referring to its concern with wealth. He sees politics as 'the master art' which must direct 'the rest of the sciences', including economics, and 'since, again, it legislates as to what we are to abstain from, the end of science must include those of the others, so that this end must be the good for man'. Furthermore, according to Sen, the study of economics, though directly related to the pursuit of wealth, is at a deeper level linked to other studies which involve the assessment and enhancement of more basic goals. Quoting Aristotle, Sen notes that, 'the life of money-making is one undertaken under compulsion, and wealth is evidently not the good we are seeking; for it is merely useful and for the sake of something else.' Economics relates ultimately to the studies of ethics and politics, a point of view further developed in Aristotle's *Politics*.[15]

The close relationship between economics and ethics had not changed much until the eighteenth century, when a Scottish academic published a book whose profound influence and impact is still very much with us today. As Ormerod has noted,[16] Adam Smith is now seen as the intellectual inspiration of the 'New Right' in Western politics. He has also exerted massive influence on the development of modern economics, with his insistence on the primacy of free-market forces and the pursuit of enlightened self-interest by individuals and companies alike.

However, before I begin to assess his contribution to the development and study of modern economics, I should like to emphasise that, as will become clearer later in this chapter, Adam Smith's ideas have been abused by those who have championed his philosophy of the free market and self-interest without embracing his other 'sentiments'. The following is a brief attempt to shed light on this observation.

Adam Smith's major economic work, which has come to be known as *The Wealth of Nations*, was published in 1776. The book, as has been observed by many, including Ormerod, 'is a tremendous analytical achievement, setting up a model of how the economy is thought to operate and further develop, while supporting the theory with an enormous sweep of contemporary and world historical evidence.'[17] It was not a piece of abstract theorising; it was, indeed, firmly rooted in reality. Adam Smith's whole purpose was to understand how economies worked, and why some countries were so much wealthier than others. The full title of the book clearly shows Smith's intention: *An Inquiry Into the Nature and Causes of the Wealth of Nations*.[18] As Ormerod points out, in the best scientific tradition, Smith observed the world, and then, and only then, sought to explain it. Observation came first, theory second.[19]

As already mentioned, *The Wealth of Nations* is not a pure eulogy of, and apology for, free-market forces or the worship of self-interest at all costs. Margaret Thatcher once infamously announced to the world, 'There is no such thing as society': such a declaration would have been completely alien to Adam Smith. One has only to study his work carefully to see that he attached great importance to the concept of society. It should not conveniently be forgotten that, before this book appeared, he was already much respected for his previous great work, *The Theory of Moral Sentiments*. Although he came to be known as 'the father of modern economics', Adam Smith was first a Professor of Moral Philosophy at the University of Glasgow.

As it has been observed, a central theme of Smith's *Moral Sentiments* was precisely to demonstrate the propensities in human nature which incline us to think about and move towards the creation of societies, sentiments such as fellow feeling and the desire to obtain the approval of others and to be worthy of that approval. Adam Smith pointed out that these sentiments crucially influence self-control and the restraint of individuals in their behaviour towards others.

Ormerod has added that self-restraint could also exist in a system in which people were motivated purely by their own self-interest, simply because of the practical value of such restraint. Life would be intolerable if everyone pursued a career of fraud, pillage and murder. Self-control, however, is not dependent upon calculated self-seeking; it is a natural, integral part of human nature.[20]

The moral climate, the dimension in which the economy and society function, is a major theme in *The Wealth of Nations*. The enlightened pursuit of self-interest is seen as the driving force behind a successful economy – but, most significantly, in the context of a shared view of what constitutes reasonable behaviour.

In conclusion, I believe, as do other observers such as Ormerod, that Adam Smith's followers generally ignore the importance to him of an overall set of values in which the economy operates. His economic theory based upon individual self-interest is remembered and celebrated, but his moral sentiments and moral framework are not. In sharp contrast to Smith, modern economists think about the economy as something which can be analysed in isolation. The institutional setting of Smith's model, historical experience and overall standards of behaviour are ruthlessly excluded from contemporary economic theory.[21] Nowhere can this misbehaviour be more clearly seen than at the headquarters of the IMF and The World Bank, where mainly American, or European economists often trained in the United States, prescribe standard American remedies to any sort of economic illness, regardless of significant differences, whether they be economic, political, institutional, racial, cultural, historical or geographical. These are points to which I shall return more fully in later chapters.

Amartya Sen, in his study of ethics and economics, has identified two main origins of economics.[22] The first relates to ethics and to an ethical view of politics, and this we have already discussed in some detail. The second relates to 'engineering' and is concerned primarily with logistical issues rather than with ultimate ends and big questions such as 'What is the good man?' or 'How should one live?' Here human behaviour is seen as being based on simple and easily characterised motives.[23] These motives are dominated by self-interest, which leads to a 'more is better' philosophy and ideas such as profit maximisation, consumption maximisation, cost minimisation and 'downsizing', to name but a few.

Because the impact and influence of the 'engineering' approach to the way economics has been studied and taught has been so enormous since the rise of Leon Walras and William Stanley Jevons in the mid-nineteenth century, I shall at this point attempt to provide a brief analysis of these ideas. It has been observed that, during the second half of the nineteenth century, economics was greatly influenced by the achievements of the physical sciences. Envious of their success and prestige, and aware of the power of mathematics and its influence on progress, economists in their droves turned to a mathematical analysis of economics.

Ormerod has discussed how, against a background of the

great achievements of physical scientists, economists sought
to emulate their work. Around 1870, quite independently of
each other, Leon Walras in Lausanne and William Stanley
Jevons at Manchester University, having both trained as phys-
icists, turned to economics and mathematical systems of analysis founded on principles used successfully in subjects such as
engineering. This remains the basis of much of modern economics. Today a great deal of the studying and teaching of
economics is the result of applying increasingly sophisticated
mathematical theory, flavoured with massive amounts of IT,
to a methodological framework.

Ormerod believes that Walras's system was the more complete of the two, and it is his name that is best remembered
in economic literature today. The phrase 'Walrasian General
Equilibrium' is one applied to the core model of economic
theory taught at universities around the world. One can argue
in summary that in many ways Walras's approach broke deci-
sively with the work of classical economists such as Adam
Smith.[24] In contrast to scholars such as Adam Smith, who took
into account specific institutional, social, political and historical factors in determining the development of any particular
economy, the new theory that was articulated was believed
to hold good for all economies at all times. I have already
commented on IMF and World Bank economists above.

As for the mathematical bias of modern economics, an
increasing number of people feel very uncomfortable when
human activities are analysed according to mathematical principles. It must not be forgotten that people like Walras were
initially interested in the working of machines – man-made
objects. Most people around the world would agree that there
is a massive difference between man-made objects and man
himself.

In contrast to modern economists the great classical economists used no mathematics, except perhaps simple arith-
metic. As a deliberate exercise, I looked through the pages of
The Wealth of Nations. This study is divided into five different
'Books' and has approximately 450 pages but it does not
contain any mathematical jargon, symbols, equations or
formulae.[25] Furthermore, Keynes, who influenced economics

more than anyone between 1930 and 1970, despite his training in mathematics allowed himself the use of no more than a few lines of elementary algebra. Indeed, one of Keynes's leading Cambridge disciples, Joan Robinson, writing in the 1950s, complained vigorously of economists hiding behind 'thickets of algebra'.[26]

A casual glance at modern academic economic journals confirms Joan Robinson's concerns. If anything, things are getting worse. Page after page, and literally whole pages, are filled with nothing but mathematical jargon and symbols. To understand articles appearing in journals such as the British *Review of Economic Studies* or the American *Econometrica*, it seems one needs a PhD in mathematics. Perhaps also a PhD in English to make sense of the text that accompanies the formulae. Professor Ormerod looked at one such article, 'Implementation in Economy with a Continuum of Agents', which contained sub-headings such as 'Upper hemicontinuity at the continuum limit' and 'Existence and Uniqueness of Equilibria when Preferences are Additively Separable'. The article makes few concessions to plain English, especially in its opening sentences:

While the infinite dimension equilibrium existence theory is now well understood, there are few results on the problem of uniqueness. The purpose of this note is to study the particular case of a pure exchange economy where agents' consumption space is Lp+(u) and agents have additively separable utilities which fulfil the hypothesis that agents' relative risk aversion coefficients are smaller than one.[27]

Who is this article trying to kid? What kind of language is this? Is this the language of the ordinary people with whom economics is supposed to be concerned? It is certainly not the language of Aristotle, Adam Smith or Keynes. It is not language in which one can explain ethics, humanity and common good. Ormerod has some answers to these questions: 'The temptation to use mathematics is irresistible for economists. It appears to convey the appropriate air of scientific authority and precision to economists' musings.'[28]

By adhering so slavishly to mathematics, much of the richness, challenge and engaging nature of the original analysis of economics have been lost. For example, Adam Smith's

awareness of an institutional framework and set of moral values in which free markets operate have largely been neglected.
As Ormerod has noted, such concepts do not readily convert
into the language of mathematics.[29]

Neo-classical economics, which has been dominant for half
a century or so, has brought to humanity a catastrophically
bitter harvest. On this, in conclusion, I should like to shed
more light.

The neo-classical economists cannot take the credit for our
buoyant market economy, however much they boast of it. As
Mason Gaffney has observed, the North Atlantic nations had
a well-oiled market economy long before neo-classical
economics drove out classical and progressive economics.
What can neo-classical economists claim as their heritage?
What is their contribution to our well-being?

They have indeed achieved power; they have implemented
much of their programme. They have dismantled most of the
reforms of the progressive era and discredited its rationale.
They have successfully encouraged the deregulation of utilities, railways, airlines and the telecommunications industry.
They have achieved the privatisation of much of what used to
be in the public domain, which had belonged to all of us, without compensation to the public. They have turned the banks
loose to lend to us – here as well as in the Third World – and
bailed them out when they failed. They have nullified progressive era electoral reforms by pouring money into politics
and 'deep lobbying', and have poured ever more taxpayers'
money into private prisons to uphold law and order.

They have encouraged a falling share for labour in the
national income, while increasing the share of property
owners. They have reduced real wages, especially in the
public sector and for the youth and female workers, while at
the same time hugely increasing the salaries, bonuses and
benefits of the heads of the newly privatised industries and
international financial institutions such as those in Wall Street
and the City.

Under the stewardship of neo-classical economists unemployment has risen to chronically high levels. Their theories
are unable to explain these catastrophic rises, so they are

continually moving the goalposts, redefining and increasing the 'natural' or 'normal' rate of unemployment from 2% to 3%, 6%, 11% ... Joblessness becomes a personal choice in the neo-classical economic cant: 'To explain why people allocate time to ... unemployment, we need to know why they prefer it to all other activities'. To more enlightened neo-classicists the unemployed are engaged in a vital economic function, 'job search'![30]

Under such leadership the number of homeless has risen sharply. In some economists' eyes these people have a 'taste' for sleeping over heating grates, in doorways, under motorways, in cardboard boxes. Perhaps they are engaged in the vital economic function of 'home search'. It is argued that they are guided by 'rational expectations'. Otherwise they are 'mentally disturbed': irrationality puts one outside the neo-classical economic system.

Because of these economic policies, hunger and beggary, once rare in the First World, are now everywhere, even in the midst of great wealth, new technology and universal education – despite all the neo-classical economists' panaceas which are supposed to create jobs. One might call this 'Progress and Poverty': more on this point later.

A common neo-classical answer to these economic problems is to sack workers in what is called 'downsizing' of the labour force, which is supposed to make an industry 'leaner and meaner'. 'Efficiency' and 'productivity' have become synonymous with lay-offs. Neo-classical economists argue that at some future date this will create new jobs by making us more 'competitive'.[31] One is reminded of Schumpeter's confidence in the power of capitalism to eliminate poverty and want – which every honest observer would agree is a huge embarrassment today.[32]

It is worth remembering that this downsizing of the labour force takes place with no regard to the well-being of the sacked workers, their families and their communities. This is not surprising: I have already argued in this study that modern economics has no interest in ethics and morality. Such concepts cannot be measured or quantified in mathematical models, however complicated. Neo-classical economics is based on greed, on the maximising of profits and the minimising of costs (if necessary by sacking the workers). 'Numbers' matter, not people.

Under the tyranny of neo-classical economics the world has lost a sense of community. As Gaffney has so eloquently argued, there is little place for a sense of public service, or honour, or loyalty, or duty, or devotion, or responsibility, in a world which is cynical of such values. The family, a communistic unit, is becoming an anachronism. It is individuals, motivated by self-interest, who make the system work. Public servants are assumed to be moved by the same self-seeking principles. Those who think and act otherwise are fools or hypocrites. This philosophy has led to a massive rise in sleaze and corruption amongst elected politicians around the world. 'Greed is good' is the creed of neo-classical economics.[33]

Neo-classical economists tolerate the church only if it narrows its focus to individual salvation; the wider social concerns which preoccupied Moses and Jesus are not considered within its sphere. In fact almost anything public or common is suspect, be it public health, public transport, public parks, public inspection of food and drugs, public air traffic control, public utilities, public broadcasting – or the public good.[34]

Many people are beginning to question the validity and morality of this philosophy, in the face of, for example, the privatisation programmes which began in Britain in the 1980s. There has been much criticism of the privatised railways and utilities and searching questions are being asked about profits, directors' bonuses, downsizing and safety. It seems it will be only a matter of time before people revolt against such unethical behaviour.

Nowhere can the bankruptcy of neo-classical philosophy be better observed than in the worldwide mobile phone crisis, which serves as a warning of the evils of unregulated capitalism, and corporate cynicism. Will Hutton, writing in *The Observer*, has addressed this issue, and because of its significance I should like to refer to his article in some detail.[35]

Hutton begins his analysis by inviting us to imagine the chorus of criticism were a collection of state-owned companies to waste tens of billions of pounds in duplicating their efforts amid stories of fraud and epic miscalculations, and whose excesses now threatened the world with recession. Attacks in the right-wing press would have been vicious. They would have surpassed themselves in their excoriation of all things public and pleaded for privatisation and deregulation. However, when the same thing happened in the world of private enterprise, silence descended. It was left to Will Hutton and *The Observer* to try to bring some sort of sanity and sound analysis to the necessary debate.

Hutton argues that what has happened to the global telecommunications industry is a salutary lesson to those who believe that public is bad and private is good. Over the last five years, American, European and Asian telecom companies have run up a debt of more than $700bn in outbidding each other for a stake in the communications action. The industry now lies crippled with debt, and the dot-com bubble has burst. It is questionable whether they can repay their debts, and this threatens the integrity of the world banking system. There were over 100,000 telecom job losses worldwide in a ten-week period between February and April 2001.

One must question the economic rationale behind encouraging a multiplicity of mobile phone and broadband networks and the prediction of a hyper-boom. The end result will be a massive round of mergers and takeovers. We will be left with a few powerful private-sector monopolies, accountable only to their shareholders, instead of pubicly accountable companies.

Will Hutton comments that capitalism in this style does not get much more stupid. 'The irrationality and greed of the companies, their huge debt accumulation, their at times useless and unworkable technology ... is a majestic condemnation of the way unmanaged and deregulated markets work.'[36] It is unbelievably absurd that the partially privatised German and French telecom companies, along with BT and countless others, attempted simultaneously to embrace and dominate the information and communication revolution, leading to massive duplication and waste. What have they got to show for it? The three mentioned above are now, respectively, £35bn, £40bn and £30bn in debt. The bubble has burst and share prices have collapsed. What the telecom

industry worldwide has done, according to Hutton, is dupe
the investing public in a way that is close to theft. There has
been an unparalleled transfer of wealth from private investors
and the pension funds of ordinary savers into the pockets of
overpaid bankers, chief executives and directors.

Economic bankruptcy is not the only sad tale. Increasingly
troubling stories of fraud are surfacing. 'Entrepreneurs' are
proving both innovative and economical with the truth in
their attempts to cash in on the short-lived boom by disguis-
ing the frailty of their companies. Many telecom and dot-com
bosses are facing fraud charges.

The trouble, argues Will Hutton, is that because the free-
market ideology sponsored by the all-powerful Americans
taught otherwise, nobody stood up for a different concept in
which the public ownership and public construction of networks was seen as rational and economically efficient. Our
willingness to follow like lemmings has led to the telecom
debacle. And still nobody dares say the emperor has no
clothes.

As this book was going to press, the world was confronted
by yet another casualty of neo-classical economics: the fall
from grace of the energy giant, Enron. The spectacular and
disgraceful collapse of Enron, which had benefited greatly
from the main British political parties, indeed from major
politicians on both sides of the Atlantic, goes a long way to
justifying the stance I have taken in this book: there is no
alternative to relying on ethics and morality in our economic
policies if we are not to be ruled by a narrow desire to achieve
maximum short-term profit for the few.

In this chapter, to sum up, I have discussed the two origins
of economics. I have demonstrated its roots in ethics and
morality and have noted the significance of religion in embracing these values. The second strand of economics originated
in science, with the rise of engineers-turned-economists who
postulated mathematical frameworks which increasingly
intruded into the heritage of classical economics. I have noted
the bitter harvest of neo-classical economists and discussed the
harmful consequences of this change of direction. I call this a
journey from promised land to wasteland.

In future chapters I shall discuss how we can reverse this direction and once again begin the journey from wasteland to promised land.

Afterword: A Pause for Thought

The public be damned. I'm working for my stockholders.

WILLIAM VANDERBILT

It was designed to maximise returns to the treasury, not to optimise safety.

GERALD CORBETT,
former Chief Executive of Railtrack, on rail privatisation

Gary Hart the driver of the Land-Rover which caused the recent train crash near Selby in Yorkshire appeared in court last week charged with causing the death of 10 people by dangerous driving ... What is remarkable is the contrast in the speed with which the prosecution against Mr Hart has been mounted and the rather different response to the equally serious railway disasters at Southall, Ladbroke Grove and more recently, Hatfield. In all three cases, public enquiries have been instigated and – certainly in the Paddington and Hatfield cases – evidence produced of serious negligence by Railtrack and the sub-contractors it employed. To date, however, not a single official has been held responsible for the deaths, let alone prosecuted ... The moral seems to be that if you are a private individual accused of negligence resulting in multiple deaths on the railways, you will be given rather different treatment from the executives of a large and powerful public company which, unlike the private individual, is actually responsible for maintaining the highest possible standards of safety.

RICHARD INGRAMS[37]

CHAPTER 3

✳

The greatest of evil and the worst of evil is poverty.

GEORGE BERNARD SHAW

For Poverty is not merely deprivation; it means shame, degradation; the searing of the most sensitive parts of our moral and mental nature as with hot irons; the denial of the strongest impulses and the sweetest affections; the wrenching of the most vital nerves.

HENRY GEORGE[1]

The millionaires club in Britain is growing at a rate of 17% a year and now has 74,000 members ... These new rich are mostly white, male, over 35, and living in the South East ... While the rich get richer, the poor get poorer and the regional gaps become starker. The mass affluents, people with assets of £30,000-£200,000 are concentrated in London (19%), East Anglia (12%), and Yorkshire and Humberside together (11%). Only 1% of people of the affluents mass live in Merseyside, 5% in Scotland and 4% in Wales ... by the end of 1999, 26% of the British population was living in poverty, measured in terms of low income and multiple deprivations of necessities ... In 1983, 14% of households lacked three or more necessities because they could not afford them. That proportion had increased to 21% in 1990 and to over 24% by 1999...

FELICITY LAWRENCE[2]

'A fair society', R.H. Tawney, writing in *Equality* noted, requires 'not only an open road but an equal start' ... A just civilisation in which we can all be at ease with ourselves is built not on the possibility of having the right to attain happiness, but on the unequivocal right to happiness. We must spread wealth around, as Tawney saw, otherwise we reinvent the structural injustice of medieval Europe ...

friendship, solidarity and even kindness rest on the notion
that we share. As Aristotle said, there is no friendship
among the unequal.

WILL HUTTON[3]

Sweatshop Profiles: A Summary[4]

Company/ Label	Factory in China	Wages/ hour	Hours/ week	Conditions
Wal-Mart/ Kathie Lee handbags	Ya Li Handbag Ltd	$0.18- $0.28	60 plus overtime up to 16-hour shift	Forced overtime, stiff fine for refusal; overtime premium of 2.5¢ an hour. Some workers not paid for 3-4 months. 12 to a dormitory room; no benefits; no work contract.
Ralph Lauren, Ellen Tracy/ Linda Allard	Iris Fashions	$0.20	72 to 80; 12 to 15-hour shifts, 6 days a week	No union; workers paid a $0.06 per hour premium for overtime; paid $0.02 for each shirt collar sewn.
Nike and Adidas Athletic Shoes	Yue Yuen Factory	$0.19	60 to 84	Forced overtime; no overtime premiums; excessive noise pollution; fumes in the factory; no worker had heard about Nike or Adidas Corporate Code of Conduct.

Take me away from the noise of your songs; to the
melody of your harps I will not listen. But let justice roll
down like waters; and righteousness like an ever-flowing
stream.

AMOS 5: 23, 24

We begin the 21st Century with the hope that the press-
ing problems for humanity will be solved, that greed will
not get in the way of common sense and humanity.

OSCAR UGARTECHE, LIMA, PERU

There is enough for everybody's need, but not enough
for their greed.

MAHATMA GANDHI

If a free society cannot help the many who are poor, it
cannot save the few who are rich.

JOHN F. KENNEDY

CHAPTER 3

Poverty, Inequality, Injustice, Marginalisation and Exclusion: The Main Ingredients of Wasteland

I N THIS STUDY, SO FAR, I have identified the catastrophic rise and indeed the persistence of poverty, indebtedness, inequality, injustice, marginalisation and exclusion in many parts of the world, including our own, as some of the failures of modern neo-classical economics. These failures have turned our land into a wasteland and our peoples into wasted peoples. These evils cannot be allowed to be glossed over; now, at the beginning of a new millennium, they are in greatest and most serious need of closer examination. This examination will be the gist of this chapter.

Before such an examination can take place, however, it would be useful to provide a working definition of 'wasteland'. It has been observed by others that wasteland exists where the majority, namely the weak, the old, the vulnerable, the unemployed, the underdeveloped, those who grow cash-crops, live under and are exploited by the minority who own and control the land and capital. The wasteland is a land of individualism, where self-interest motivates behaviour, and self-love and self-promotion rule; a land where the private sector is accountable solely to its shareholders while the public sector, which is accountable to the community at large, is run down and becomes less and less important. It is a land where common good, solidarity and society mean very little, where there is no hope and vision of a just social order. It is a land where millions of working people, living in severe poverty, are

robbed of the fruits of their labour, and where most newly
created jobs are in low-paid, low-skilled businesses. It is a land
where people are captured and enslaved to indebtedness,
dehumanised, degraded and denied 'the strongest impulses
and the sweetest affections'.[5]

Moreover, the wasteland is a land run by neo-classical economists of the IMF and the World Bank. They give their
economic blessing to the looting and plundering of man and
nature, saying that all this makes perfect economic sense as
part of an 'austerity programme'.[6] This wasteland is indeed
a land where there are many choices; however, as Mason
Gaffney has argued, though this sounds good, liberating and
positive, in practice dealing with such complexity has become
a new and dismal science, a science of choice where most of
the choices are bad.[7]

This is a good summing up. Wasteland exists where:

- corruption and sleaze are on the increase and are becoming more difficult to curtail;
- the nation state has been weakened, and with it democracy and traditional political party influence;
- fundamentalism, including overt racism, is on the rise,
  and 'positive' ideologies are in decline;
- there is an ever-increasing polarisation of wealth, where
  the rich are being paid and rewarded more and more for
  their 'labour' while the poor are being paid less and less,
  so that they are forced to work harder and harder;
- capital, and unelected, unaccountable transnational corporations have more power than elected governments;
- illicit activities such as drug-dealing and the related
  money-laundering, is increasing;
- crucial technologies, especially information technology,
  are increasingly being controlled by fewer people;
- serious and catastrophic environmental degradation is
  taking place in the service of 'economic' efficiency, in other
  words the maximising of profits and the minimising of
  costs;

• neo-liberal economic policies have virtually achieved global ascendancy, to the detriment of the majority.[8]

Archbishop Helder Camaro once remarked, 'When I help the poor I am called a saint, but when I ask why they are poor I am called a Communist.'[9] In my view too, one need not be a communist to recognise that among the causes of wasteland is unjust economic policy.

In what follows, I will firstly attempt to provide an analysis of indebtedness and poverty in the Third World. However, these problems are not restricted to Africa, Latin America or the poorest parts of Asia. As Duchrow argues, there is also pauperisation in the United States, Britain and Germany, and other developed countries.[10] As an example of poverty in the North, I shall therefore also highlight aspects of this major scandal in Britain.

As George Ann Potter in her recent excellent and timely book, *Deeper than Debt*[11], has eloquently observed, close attention all over the world is being paid to certain major common concerns: concerns such as the world order, the existence of institutionality, yet another lost decade in Latin America, catastrophic man-made and natural disasters in Africa, major political changes in Eastern Europe and Asia, a mass international migration from the South to the North. Potter argues that corporate financial globalisation, with its own strict rules, is oppressing debtor nations, and is certainly not making the world a better place to live in.

As Kevin Watkins, writing in 1997 in *Globalisation and Liberalisation*, has noted:

globalisation encapsulates both a description of changing patterns of world trade and finance, and an overwhelming conviction that deregulated markets will achieve optimal outcomes for growth and human welfare. Seldom since the heyday of free trade in the 19th Century has economic theory inspired such certainty and never has it been so far removed from reality. Poverty, mass unemployment, and inequality have grown alongside the expansion of trade and foreign investment associated with globalisation. In the developing world, poverty continues to increase in absolute terms, and the gap between 'successful' and 'unsuccessful' countries is widening. In the industrialised world unemployment has reached levels not witnessed since the 1930s and, in some countries, income inequalities are wider than at any time this century.[12]

Once again we can see the influence of neo-classical economists who tell us, 'if it's not hurting, it's not working,' it's 'a pain worth paying for' because there is going to be 'light at the end of the tunnel'!

George Ann Potter argues that global debt and the financial crisis of the 1990s are man-made problems. This, in Potter's view (a view I strongly share) is the most essential fact to grasp in the complex set of issues which confronts the world economy today. The problems that have been created are human problems and they are having a disastrous effect on the poor everywhere in the world. They are man-made problems for which neo-classical economic policies are responsible and they are deliberately designed to keep the indebted in debt bondage.

Economic policies are based on the desire for profits; economic decisions are motivated by greed and self-interest, they are not taken for the good of the people at large. Hunger, poor health, bad housing and education, decreasing employment opportunities, loss of sovereignty, a lack of emotional satisfaction, loneliness, depression, anxiety, drug and alcohol abuse – these are the consequences of national economies struggling with debt and globalisation.[13]

In a recent United Nations publication on the global distribution of income, it was noted that the richest 20% of the world's population received 82.7% of the world's income, while the poorest 20% received only 1.4%. After so many decades of economic development, industrialisation, modernisation and globalisation, global economic prosperity has rarely filtered down to the poorest. In another study it was noted that the richest 360 people on the planet own as much wealth as the poorest two billion. What this means is that, globally, we have a situation of economic apartheid in which the proportion of the haves to the have-nots is roughly 1 to 4. Consider also global energy consumption, CO_2 emissions, the amount of waste produced, pollution and other environmental factors, and it becomes clear that the same 20% of the global population is also responsible for some 80% of the forces of destruction of our planet.

As well as the creation of economic apartheid the last half century since Bretton Woods has also witnessed a massive rise in the indebtedness of the poor South to the rich North. In a recent UN report it was stated that creditor banks in affluent countries extracted from indebted countries $50bn annually in debt servicing alone. As a result of the present rules governing world markets, poor countries lose at least $500bn annually to rich countries. This is nearly ten times as much as they receive annually in aid!

In many parts of the South a point of terrible misery has been reached. More and more people are finding it impossible to acquire their basic human needs, food, clothing and shelter. For us in the North, faced with so many images of the starving millions, children and adults alike, these people are becoming mere statistics. In many parts of the South people talk about the 'decomposing' of societies, meaning their fragmentation into ungovernable factions. These are sometimes called 'post catastrophic societies'.[14] Nowhere can this phenomenon be better observed than in Africa, where the plight and struggles of many African peoples has been highlighted by both academics and the mass media.

Today, many parts of Africa, although rich in human as well as natural resources, remain among the poorest regions of the world, with the highest debt burdens in the world. Half of Africa's peoples live in abject poverty and are subjected to occasional famine. Economic conditions for the majority – despite so-called deregulated free-trade globalisation – have been getting increasingly worse over the last twenty-five years. It has been argued that the greatest barrier to economic recovery is the region's overwhelming debt burden, which amounts to some $230bn. Expressing the total external debt as a percentage of GNP, the debt burden of sub-Saharan Africa is around 83%, compared to Latin America's 36%.

No fewer than 33 of the region's 44 countries are designated 'heavily indebted poor countries' while the rest very nearly qualify for that ranking. The creditors, chiefly the IMF and World Bank, impose harsh conditions known as 'austerity programmes' with catastrophic consequences for already impoverished and vulnerable people.

Much of this debt was accumulated by African countries in the 1970s, a time of reckless lending by Northern banks and international agencies. Most if not all of these loans were taken out by illegitimate, unelected, unaccountable, undemocratic regimes. In many cases the ordinary people of Africa realised no benefits as the money disappeared into failed infrastructure projects, corrupt schemes, massive arms imports or unwise investments benefiting mainly the creditor countries.

All of this has a very important historical parallel elsewhere, and it is useful to remember it. As Oscar Ugarteche has noted,[15] only two countries in history have reneged on international debts: the Soviet Union and the United States. The rest have had to live with past mistakes. When the United States had problems with unpaid bonds on the London Market, and were unwilling to reach an agreement, the United Kingdom appealed to an international board of arbitration at the League of Nations in the late 1920s. However, to the dismay of the British government, this initiative was vetoed by the US Congress to which it was referred for ratification. They argued that there had been a referendum in Mississippi in 1852 in which the population had voted against repaying the debt because they did not know how it had been raised or how the money had been used. This decision was later incorporated into the United States Constitution as a Constitutional Amendment of 1890.

Given this historical precedent, it could surely be argued that the Third World debtor nations should be entitled to hold referendums in which their people could legitimately express the opinion that their debts should be cancelled because they did not know how they were raised or how the money was used! If this were to happen one could only wonder at the reaction of President Bush, with his 'compassionate', 'faith-based', conservatism, or of the neo-classical economists who have encouraged us to believe that these debts were necessary in order to achieve accelerated growth and overcome poverty.

In 1996 sub-Saharan Africa (excluding South Africa) paid $2.5bn more in debt servicing than it received in new long-term loans and credit. The IMF alone has taken more than $3bn out of Africa since the mid-1980s. In 1997, for example, it received $600m more than it put in. As George Ann Potter argues, it is the poor people of the indebted countries, those who have benefited least, who end up paying the price as scarce resources are diverted to debt servicing and through the effects of the IMF and World Bank austerity programmes.[16]

This was all happening at a time when Africa's export prices had been falling by an average of 1.2% each year during the 1990 to 1996 period, while import prices increased significantly. If Africa's export prices had kept pace with import prices since 1980, then, it has been argued, Africa could have repaid all its debts one-and-a-half times over.[17]

Given this enormous problem, while saluting the great work done by fundraising organisations worldwide, we must also ask them to publicise the urgent need for global economic change, the need for fair trade rather than free trade. We must bring to an end the current model of development, based on the dominant neo-classical paradigm, which has done so little to end world poverty. On the contrary, it has caused much pain and suffering in both South and North. Some aspects of the development of Third World countries, and the evils of uncontrolled, unaccountable free trade (especially the arms trade) have been addressed in some detail by me in two previous publications, to which the interested reader is invited to refer.[18]

Nowadays economic apartheid exists not only between North and South, but also within the North itself. The following is an attempt to discuss this further: poverty in Britain today is taken as an example of poverty in the North.

Recently two important publications, by the Joseph Rowntree Foundation and the Department of Social Security respectively, have clearly and convincingly demonstrated the extent of inequality, poverty and social exclusion in Britain today.[19] I shall briefly highlight some of their findings.

The studies report that, although there was significant economic growth in the years before the 1997 General Election, the proportion of people living in poverty (on below half the average income) rose to 24% in 1995-7 or 14.1m people, an increase of 9.1m on 1979. More than a third (34%) of all children, 4.6m, lived below this poverty level, 3.2m more than in 1979. Much of the increase in the number of people living in low income households resulted from the growth in the number of working-age households where no one was in work. Nearly 20% of working-age households had no working adult.

Income inequalities grew dramatically between 1979 and the early 1990s, and, following a slight reversal after 1992-3, they have started to rise again. While real average income rose by 44% between 1979 and 1995-7, the income of the poorest 10% fell by 9%. The next poorest 40% saw their incomes rise between 5% and 31%, well below the average. On the other hand, households with above average incomes have enjoyed rapid and accelerated increases. Those in the top half of the income distribution scale had rises of more than 40%, with the income of the richest 10% rising by a massive 70%. In 1979 the richest 10% had more than four times the income of the poorest 10%; by 1995-7 this had risen to nearly eight times. Between 1979 and 1995-7 the share of the total income taken by the top 10% had risen from 21% to 27%, while the share of the poorest 10% had fallen from 4% to 2.2%. At the same time the share of the top 50% had risen from 68% to 75%, while the share of the bottom 50% had fallen from 32% to 25%.

The divisions in society indicated by these statistics are almost certainly an underestimation. They do not cover the whole population. Excluded from the survey are people in residential care, and homeless people in bed-and-breakfast accommodation or sleeping rough. At the other end of the scale there is a shortfall of investment income at the top levels when compared with National Accounts, so income at the top levels of income distribution is understated.

Finally, it should be noted that the relatively high standards of living of many working-class and middle-class families have been achieved largely at the expense of personal, social and family life. There has been a growth in the number of two-earner households; many people are working longer hours and doing evening and weekend work. 1.2m people have two jobs – two thirds of them women – almost double the level of

1984. British workers work the longest hours in the European Union, with one third working more than a 48-hour week. The average weekly overtime worked by full-time workers has increased from four to seven hours for men and from three to six hours for women since 1988. One in two working men and one in three working women work some or most Sundays and one in six workers now works in the evenings as well as during the day.

In conclusion, in this chapter an attempt has been made to identify and describe wasteland. I have argued that wasteland exists where inequality, injustice, indebtedness, social exclusion and marginalisation are found in abundance. Self-centred, North-inspired and implemented globalisation, and the reliance on neo-classical economic policies, has resulted in the catastrophic indebtedness and poverty of the Third World.

I have also observed that wasteland is not confined to the Third World; it is also to be found in the First World. I highlighted the case of modern Britain as an example of what is taking place in the rich countries of the North. Finally, I have argued that, unless there are fundamental changes in global economic policies, especially in areas of trade and financial flow, and a new approach to global development (very different from the dominant neo-classical paradigm), there will be little to help the majorities in the North as well as in the South.

Afterword: A Pause for Thought
on the IMF and the World Bank

THIS AFTERWORD is based largely on the reflections of Joseph Stiglitz, ex-chief economist at the World Bank. He had also been Chairman of President Clinton's Council of Economic Advisors. The World Bank fired him two years ago: he was excommunicated simply for expressing mild dissent from World Bank views on globalisation. He recently gave an interview in *The Observer* (29th April 2001) and, because of its significance to this study, I should like to discuss it here.

Stiglitz helped *The Observer* to decode and assimilate a cache of 'confidential' and 'restricted' documents which revealed the inside workings of the IMF, the World Bank and the bank's 51% owner, the US Treasury. One such document was a 'country assistance strategy'. There is allegedly a different assistance strategy for every poorer nation, designed by the World Bank after careful local investigation. However, according to Stiglitz, this 'investigation' involves little more than the close inspection of five-star hotels. It concludes with a meeting with the begging finance minister, who is handed a pre-drafted 'restructuring agreement' for 'voluntary' signature. Each nation's economy is analysed, says Stiglitz, and then the Bank hands every minister the same four-step programme.

Step one is privatisation. Far from objecting to the selling-off of state industries, some politicians – using the World Bank's demands to silence local critics – happily dispose of their electricity and water companies. 'You could see their eyes widen at the possibility of commissions for shaving a few billion off the sale price.'

Stiglitz argues that the US government was aware of this, as in the case of the biggest privatisation of all, the 1995 Russian sell-off. The US Treasury view was, says Stiglitz, 'This was great, as we wanted Yeltsin to be re-elected. We don't care if it's a corrupt election.' Most sickening in his view was that US-backed oligarchs stripped Russia of its industrial assets; the effect was that national output was nearly cut in half.

After privatisation, step two is capital market liberalisation. In theory this allows investment capital to flow in and out.

Unfortunately, as in Indonesia and Brazil, money often simply flows out. Stiglitz calls this the 'hot money' cycle. Cash comes in for speculation in real estate and currency, then flees at the first whiff of trouble. A nation's reserves can be drained away in days.

When this happens, to seduce speculators into returning the nation's own capital funds, the IMF demands that these nations raise their interest rates – to 30%, 50% or even 80%. The result is predictable, says Stiglitz. High interest rates demolish property values, savage industrial production and drain national treasuries.

At this point of desperation, the IMF drags the gasping nation to step three: market-based pricing – a fancy term for raising prices on essential items such as food, water and gas for cooking. This leads predictably to step three-and-a-half: what Stiglitz calls 'the IMF riot'.

The IMF riot is painfully predictable. When a nation is 'down and out' the IMF squeezes the last drop of blood out of it. To change the metaphor, they turn up the heat until, finally, the whole cauldron blows up. This was best seen when the IMF eliminated food and fuel subsidies for the poor of Indonesia in 1998 and the whole country exploded into riots. Other examples include the Bolivian riots over water prices in 2001 and the February 2001 riots in Ecuador over the rise in cooking gas prices imposed by the World Bank.

A pattern emerges, argues Stiglitz: there are lots of losers but the clear winners are the Western banks and the US Treasury. At this point of misery we arrive at step four: free trade.

This is not in fact free trade for everyone, this is free trade according to the rules of the World Trade Organisation and the World Bank, which Stiglitz likens to the Opium Wars: those too were about 'opening markets'. As in the 19th Century, Europeans and Americans today are breaking down barriers to trade with Asia, Latin America and Africa, while barricading their own markets against Third World agricultural and other imports. In the Opium Wars the West used military blockades; today the World Bank can order a financial blockade that is just as effective and sometimes just as deadly.

Stiglitz has two concerns about the IMF/World Bank plans. Firstly, he says, because they are devised in secrecy and are driven by an absolutist ideology, never open to discussion or dissent, they 'undermine democracy'. Secondly, they don't work. Under the guiding hand of IMF structural 'assistance' Africa's income has dropped by 23%.

Stiglitz proposes radical land reform: an attack on the 50% crop rents charged by the propertied oligarchies worldwide. Why didn't the World Bank and the IMF follow his advice? asks *The Observer*. 'If you challenge [land ownership], that would be a change in the power of the elites.' 'That's not high on their agenda,' replies Stiglitz.

He concludes his interview by saying that, ultimately, what drove him to put his job on the line was the failure of the banks and the US Treasury to change course when confronted with the crises and failures, and the suffering perpetrated by their four-step monetarist mambo. 'It's a little like the Middle Ages, when the patient died they would say, well, we stopped the bloodletting too soon, he still had a little blood in him.'

Second Pause for Thought:
World Bank Can't Afford Debt Write-off

DROP THE DEBT, the successor organisation to Jubilee 2000, on 27th April 2001 urged the World Bank and the IMF to write off the debts crippling countries in Africa and Latin America. However, in response to this request, James Wolfensohn, President of the World Bank, maintained that the Bank couldn't afford to ignore the remaining debts of the poorest nations. He said a total write-off for these 63 developing countries would cost $29bn, an impossible price to pay.

We need to consider this statement alongside the decision of George Bush's government to cut US taxes – for the benefit mainly of the super-rich – by 1.3 *trillion* dollars. Bearing in mind Stiglitz's comment that much of the debt repayment is swelling US Treasury coffers, the question for the rest of the world is: Is this ethical or moral?

Third Pause for Thought:
A Note on the Origin of the IMF
and the World Bank

THE INVESTIGATIVE JOURNALIST and campaigner John Pilger, writing in the *New Statesman* (9th July 2001) notes that:

It was the triumphant American state that fashioned the present 'global economy' at Bretton Woods in 1944, so that its military and corporate aims would have unlimited access to minerals, oil, markets and cheap labour. In 1948, the State Department's senior imperial planner, George Kennan, wrote: 'We have 50% of the world's wealth, but only 6.3% of its population. In this situation, our real job in the coming period is to devise a pattern of relationships which permit us to maintain this position of disparity. To do so, we have to dispense with all sentimentality ... we should cease thinking about human rights, the raising of living standards and democratisation.' The World Bank and the International Monetary Fund (IMF) were invented to implement this strategy. Their base is in Washington, where they are joined by an umbilical cord to the US Treasury, a few blocks away. This is where the globalisation of poverty and the use of debt as a weapon of control was conceived. When John Maynard Keynes, the British representative at Bretton Woods, proposed a tax on creditor nations, designed to prevent poor countries falling into perpetual debt, he was told by the Americans that if he persisted, Britain would not get its desperately needed war loans. More than half a century later, the gap between the richest 20% of humanity and the poorest 20% has doubled, and 'structural adjustment programmes' have secured an indebted imperium greater than the British Empire at its height.

A pertinent question for the rest of the world is: Given their origin and historical development, can we expect that the IMF, World Bank, and more recently created WTO, change their spots and become like an institutional Mother Teresa, with a 'mission to defeat poverty'? Only the reader can answer this question.

CHAPTER 4

It is intolerable that the most important issues about human livelihood will be decided solely on the basis of profit for transnational corporations.

HERMAN E. DALY & JOHN B. COBB JR[1]

The revolt against capitalism has its sources, not merely in material miseries, but in resentment against an economic system which dehumanises existence by treating the mass of mankind not as responsible partners in the co-operative enterprise of subduing nature to the service of man, but as instruments to be manipulated for the pecuniary advantage of a minority of property-owners.

R.H. TAWNEY[2]

Within economic theory and the market it promotes, the moral dimension of greed is inevitably lost; today it seems left to religion to preserve what is problematic about a human trait that is unsavoury at best and unambiguously evil at its worst.

DAVID R. LOY[3]

CHAPTER 4

Common Good, Solidarity,
Justice, Love, Faith and Hope:
The Main Ingredients
of the Promised Land

IN CHAPTER 3 we travelled through many inhospitable lands, through many deserts in what we called the wasteland. In this chapter, we travel through many oases and pleasant lands in an attempt to reach the promised land.

When terms such as 'promised land', 'common good', 'solidarity' and 'faith' are used, they are generally left unexplained, as though their meanings were evident to everyone. In reality, it seems that this is not the case. It appears that many people of goodwill use these terms because they sound good and ethical but without any deeper understanding of their implications. In this chapter, my main task will be to correct this perceived shortcoming, explaining the terms we take for granted.

1 Promised Land

IN MY VIEW, to understand what the promised land is, and its relevance to economics and social ethics, one should look no further than the Bible itself.

In the Bible, according to Andelson and Dawsey[4], the promised land is described as the 'eminent domain' of God. After forty years in the wasteland, when a new generation was ready to enter the land across the Jordan, Joshua reminded his people of how the Lord had given them the land which bore fruit and olives, and before them he made a covenant with God, saying, 'as for me and my house, we will serve the Lord' (*Josh.* 24: 13-15). However, the promised land is not so much a geographical place as a goal and vision – the dream of a just social order. When Jesus said, 'Blessed are you poor, for yours is the kingdom of God' (*Luke* 6: 20; cf. *Matt.* 5: 3), he was affirming the justice of God's reign. Jesus was saying that the poor can be of good comfort in God's kingdom because there they will not be exploited.

We should note that Jesus held the same view as the prophets as to what caused poverty. For the prophets, poverty was the consequence of human exploitation. Nowhere is this clearer than when Amos called forth destruction upon Israel:

> because they sell the righteous for silver, and the needy for a pair of shoes – they that trample the head of the poor into the dust of the earth and turn aside the way of the afflicted.
>
> *Amos* 2: 6-7

Andelson and Dawsey argue[5] that Jesus was simply affirming his view of poverty when he paired the beatitudes with woes in *Luke* 6: 20-26. Jesus cursed the rich because, like Amos, he saw the connection between rich men's wealth and the misery of the poor. For Jesus, as for Amos and the other prophets, righteousness involves a right relationship between people, and also right actions which lead to wellbeing.

Jeremiah observed that if people would 'execute justice one with another' then God would let them dwell in the land that he gave of old to the fathers forever (*Jer.* 7: 5-7). Justice – and this cannot be over-emphasised – is essential to the creation of the promised land.[6]

The biblical meanings of 'justice' are many, but what are the essential characteristics of doing justice that pertain directly to this study?

To do justice means to perceive and be responsive to the needs of the community as a whole, as Paul pointed out to the Corinthian Christians. He reminded them that God's righteousness consists of scattering his abundance abroad, giving to the poor (*2 Cor.* 9: 9-10), and making God's bounty (or natural opportunity) available to all.[7] This, according to Andelson and Dawsey, helps explain why the early Church held possessions in common. Those who possessed property felt responsible for those in need. Therefore, 'there was not a needy person among them, for as many as were possessors of lands or houses sold them, and brought the proceeds of what was sold and laid it at the apostles' feet; and distribution was made to each as any had need' (*Acts* 4: 34-35). There was no room for accumulating excess or for holding land unproductive and hoarding it as a personal reserve of wealth. As Ananias and Sapphira found out, to hold back the proceeds of the land from the community was to cheat God (*Acts* 5: 3).

As noted earlier, modern economics emphasises individuals and their private gains; it does not pay any attention to the significance of community and common good. It is worth observing what, in contrast, the promised land has to offer.

Andelson and Dawsey[8] note that although the Promised Land does offer individuals opportunities for private gain, it does so only within the framework of opportunities for the community as a whole to live and work under God's reign, in harmony with the land and with each other:

Now, not every kind of distribution of wealth and prosperity among men is such that it can satisfactorily, still less adequately, attain the end intended by God. Wealth therefore, which is constantly being augmented by social and economic progress, must be so distributed among the individuals and classes of society that the common good of all, of which Leo XIII spoke, be thereby promoted. In other words, the good of the whole community must be safeguarded. Each class, then, must receive its due share, and the distribution of created goods must be brought into conformity with the demands of the common good and social justice. For every sincere observer realises that the vast differences between the few who hold excessive wealth and the many who live in destitution constitute a grave evil in modern society.[9]

With this in mind, the words of Pope Pius XI, in his encyclical letter of 1931, are most heartening:

Free competition ... cannot be the guiding principle of economic life. Nor can dictatorship, domination, or excessive economic or financial power, public or private; nor mere individualism, profit and wealth by all and any means, a lawless market, and the survival of the strongest ... The guiding principles for our lives and work must be justice and – above all – love; individual and social ... Authority should foster a society inspired with these principles, and should see that we keep our

competition and power within just limits. We must reform our conduct, and give priority to the moral rather than the material. Excessive
concern for money or possessions blocks growth of heart and mind.[10]

John Paul II, in the context of 'Development and Freedom',
has eloquently observed:

Development that is merely economic, that ignores our cultural,
transcendent and religious dimensions, cannot set human beings free:
it will end by enslaving us further. We are free only when we are
completely ourselves, in the fullness of our rights and duties.[11]

The promised land, in a nutshell, is a land abundant in
justice, love, compassion, sympathy, empathy, a sense of community, sharing and caring. It is not a land of individualism,
self-interest, greed, materialism, unethical behaviour, sleaze
and corruption. Given this, we cannot deny that today we live
in a globalised wasteland.

As I have stressed again and again in this study, it is my
view that economics, as developed in modern times and taught
in our universities and other places of higher education, bears
the major responsibility for creating and maintaining this
wasteland. To achieve the liberating potentials of the promised land, modern economics must change. It has to become
more community oriented and more in harmony with true
human values. To begin to achieve this, a better understanding of the religion of the marketplace is a necessary first step.
This is the topic to which I shall now turn.

2 Economics as Theology

IN CHAPTER 3 aspects of abject poverty, with its accom-
panying shame, degradation, dehumanisation and injustice,
both in the poor South and the rich North, were highlighted
and discussed. To endorse my observations in that chapter, I
repeat David Loy's questions in his own study of this subject[12]:
'Why do we acquiesce in this social injustice?' and 'What
rationalisation allows us to sleep peacefully at night?'

The explanation lies largely in our embrace of a peculiarly European or Western [but now global] religion, an individualistic religion of economics and markets, which explains all of these outcomes as the inevitable results of an objective system in which intervention is counterproductive. Employment is simply a cost of doing business, and Nature is merely a pool of resources for use in production. In this calculus, the world of business is so fundamental and so separate from the environment that intervention in the ongoing economic system is a threat to the natural order of things, and hence to future human welfare. In this way of thinking, that outcome is just (or at least inevitable) which emerges from the natural workings of this economic system, and the 'wisdom of the market' on which it is based. The hegemony achieved by this particular intellectual construct – a 'European religion' or 'economic religion' – is remarkable; it has become a dogma of almost universal application, the dominant religion of our time, shoring up and justifying what would appear to be a patently inequitable status quo. It has achieved an immense influence, which dominates contemporary human activity.[13]

According to Dobell, as quoted by Loy, this theology is based on two counterintuitive but widely accepted propositions: that it is right and just (which is why 'the market made me do it' is acceptable as a defence of many morally questionable activities), and that value can adequately be signalled by prices. The basic assumption of both propositions, argues Loy, is that such a system is 'natural'. If market capitalism does operate according to economic laws as natural as those of physics or chemistry – if economics were a genuine science – its consequences are apparently unavoidable, despite the fact that they are leading to extreme social inequity, and environmental degradation and catastrophe.

However, there is in fact nothing inevitable about our economic relationships. This misunderstanding, according to Loy, is exactly what we need to address – and this is also where religion comes in, since, with the increasing prostitution of the media as well as our universities to these same market forces, there appears to be no other moral perspective left from which to challenge them. Fortunately, as has been observed, the alternative world-views that religions offer can still help us realise that the global victory of market capitalism is something other than the attainment of economic freedom: rather, it is the ascendancy of one particular way of understanding and valuing the world that need not be taken for granted.[14]

What is most impressive about market values from a religious perspective is not, argues Loy, their 'naturalness' but how extraordinarily persuasive their conversion techniques are. Compare and contrast the limited success that religions in general have had in converting people to their respective belief systems with the infinitely greater success of global market-oriented values and principles. With an annual conversion budget of hundreds of billions of dollars (i.e. worldwide advertising), globalised market values are the only truly successful worldwide 'religion'. Their sometimes very attractive (often hypnotic, and most of the time sexy and sensuous) advertising messages on our televisions and radios, in our magazines, newspapers, buses and trains, constantly proselytise new converts to the icons of capitalism and the free-market economy. In contrast to most traditional religions which promise happiness in the after life, they go one step further and promise constant happiness in the here and now: 'Buy me if you want to be happy' is their main message. If we are not blinded by the distinction usually made between secular and sacred, we can see that this promises another kind of salvation, another way to solve our unhappiness.[15]

According to Loy, the scholar who did the most to uncover the religious roots of market capitalism was Max Weber. His controversial theory not only locates the origins of capitalism in the 'this-worldly ascetism' of Puritan ethics but also suggests that capitalism remains essentially religious in its psychological structure. Another study, which concentrates on Calvinism, examines the belief in predestination which encouraged what became an irresistible need to determine whether one was among the chosen. Here, says Loy, economic success in this world came to be accepted as demonstrating God's favour. This created the psychological and sociological conditions for importing ascetic values from the monastery into worldly vocations, as one laboured to prove oneself saved by reinvesting any surplus rather than consuming it. Over time this original goal gradually weakened, and yet inner-worldly asceticism did not disappear as God became more distant and heaven less relevant.

In this modern world of ours, Loy notes, the original motivation has evaporated but our preoccupation with capital and profit has not disappeared with it; it has indeed become our main obsession. 'Since we no longer have any other goal, there being no other final salvation to believe in, we allow the means to be, in effect, our end.'[16] Polanyi in *The Great Transformation* states, 'We no longer give our surplus to God; the process of producing an ever-expanding surplus is in itself our God.'[17]

Loy argues that, in contrast to the cyclical timescale of premodern societies with their seasonal rituals of atonement, our economic time is linear and future-oriented. It reaches towards an atonement that can no longer be achieved because it has disappeared as a conscious motivation. However, as a subconscious incentive it still exists: we continue to strive for an end that is perpetually postponed. Our collective reaction has become the desire for improvement, the never-satisfied yearning for an ever-higher 'standard of living'. Once we declare ourselves as consumers, we can never have too much. Hence the gospel of sustained economic expansion, because corporations and the GNP are never big enough.[18]

David Loy eloquently brings these points together when he says:

... our humanity reduced to a source of labour and a collection of insatiable desires, as our communities disintegrate into aggregates of individuals competing to attain private ends ... the earth and all its creatures' commodified into a pool of resources to be exploited to satisfy those desires ... does this radical dualism leave any place for the sacred? For wonder and awe before the mysteries of creation? Whether or not we believe in God, we may suspect that something is missing. Here we are reminded of the crucial role that religions can serve: to raise fundamental questions about this diminished understanding of what the world is and what our life can be.[19]

Looking at the problem of market capitalism and its values from a religious perspective, it has been suggested that these can be identified as twofold: namely, greed and delusion. Within the domains of economic theory and the kind of market it promotes, the moral concept of greed has inevitably been lost: 'today it seems left to religion to preserve what is problematic about a human trait that is unsavoury at best and unambiguously evil at its worst.' Religious traditions have tended to accept greed as part of the human condition, but rather than give it free reign they have seen a great need to control it.

Spiritually speaking, the problem with greed – both the greed for profit and the greed to consume – is not only that it results in the maldistribution of worldly goods, or that it adversely affects the environment, but more profoundly because greed, as Loy has argued, is fundamentally based on a delusion: the delusion that happiness is to be found this way.

Trying to find fulfilment through profit, or by making consumption the meaning of one's life, amounts to idolatry, that is, a demonic perversion of true religion; and any religious institution that makes its peace with the priority of such market values does not deserve the name of genuine religion.[20]

We are unlikely ever to solve the problem of social justice without also seeing through the delusion that happiness can result from selfish accumulation and consumption, if only because of the ability of those who control the world's resources to manipulate things to their own perceived advantage.

The greed and delusion which are fundamental to the workings and values of the global marketplace have destructively affected the way in which we see ourselves and relate to others. With the breakdown of community at all levels, human beings have become more like what the traditional model of *Homo economicus* described. Shopping has become the great national pastime … On the basis of massive borrowing and massive sales of national assets, Americans have been squandering their heritage and impoverishing their children.[21]

Furthermore, in an attempt to satisfy this ever-increasing but never-to-be-satisfied greed we have especially over the last half century achieved the virtual destruction of our environment. According to the Worldwatch Institute, more goods and services have been consumed by people living between 1950 and 1990 (measured in constant dollars) than by all the previous generations in human history.[22] So much for our patrimony.

As Loy notes, our extraordinary wealth has not been enough for us: we have supplemented it by accumulating extra-ordinary amounts of debt.

How ingenious we have been to devise an economic system that allows us to steal from the assets of our descendants! Our commodifications have enabled us to achieve something usually believed impossible, time-travel: we now have ways to colonize and exploit even the future.[23]

The above observations should come as no surprise to those with a more traditional religious orientation to the world. By far the best critique of this greed for consumption is provided by the traditional religions such as Buddhism, Hinduism, Judaism, Christianity and Islam. They all offer a wealth of teachings and recommendations as to how we should ethically and morally lead our lives, and how we can achieve happiness away from greed and delusion.[24]

In conclusion, as Loy wisely observes, the free market is not just an economic system but also a religion, and for that matter not a very good one: it can thrive only by promising a secular salvation that it never supplies. Its academic discipline, the 'social science' of economics, is much better understood as a theology pretending to be a science.[25]

This suggests that any solution to the problems created by the free market must also have a religious dimension. That is why, in this book, I am attempting to concentrate my analysis on the solutions provided by the Catholic church, as an example of what traditional religions as a whole have to offer.

3 A Catholic Perspective on Justice Theory

IN THIS STUDY, so far, an attempt has been made clearly to highlight the evils of poverty, inequality, injustice, greed, conspicuous consumption, marginalisation and exclusion. There are many perspectives from which it is possible to analyse these problems. However, as Fr Alberto Munera, SJ has observed[26], in the Roman Catholic perspective of liber-ation theology there is only one: 'These problems must be considered and interpreted in terms of justice theory from the perspective of the poor and the oppressed.' This perspective includes poor people and also the poor embattled earth, our wasteland.

Liberation theology has its roots in the biblical traditions of Judaism and Christianity, and also in the traditional social and distributive justice theory that grew up in Catholic moral teaching. The plight and daily struggles of the poor, their dehumanisation, marginalisation and exclusion, as well as the greed of the marketplace and environmental degradation, are all due to unjust economic systems and structures, and their supporting ideologies sustained by the rich for their own benefit.[27]

A Catholic approach to this problem must be taken from the same perspective that Jesus clearly demonstrated in his daily dealing with the poor, the oppressed, the marginalised, the weak, the rejected, and those considered the debris of this world. This approach calls for a perspective of deep knowledge of the concrete situations and a religious reaction of justice – love that requires an effective praxis capable of transforming such a terrible reality. Liberation theology's justice theory requires all of this.[28]

Fr Munera writes:

From my perspective of living and working in the poor part of the world [Bogotá, Columbia], I can see that the main problem is the rapaciousness of the rich with their insatiable consuming patterns. The economically powerful have all the possibilities of acquiring lands and goods and of transforming any kind of resources for their own benefit, and more importantly, they are also the producers and owners of technology. What can the poor do in this absolutely unequal and unjust competition for consumption, in what is blithely called 'the global economy?[29]

It has been argued that the concept of need is the key to Catholic economic theory and to any biblical theory of justice, but it has no status at all in global capitalism. For global capitalism is 'the rule of the greedy, for the greedy, by the greedy'.

Large financial institutions like the World Bank and the IMF, as well as unelected, unaccountable, transnational corporations, Fr Munera points out, have enormous power. However, the result of this power is not benign for the poor.

Workers and indeed whole populations are constantly brutalised by unjust 'austerity' requirements to meet perhaps 'illegal' debts (see Chapter 3) to the rich First World.

Furthermore, and even more seriously, these institutions do not show any interest in ecology. Being ecologically prudent does not in the short term produce money, the oxygen of capitalism.

When the only objective is to produce money in great quantities quickly, it does not matter if that production presupposes the destruction of the earth's resources. That they are sawing the limb on which they sit seems not to occur to them.[30]

This self-interested and unethical behaviour is well demonstrated by the newly 'appointed' US President's decision in the interests of giant American oil and coal producers unilaterally to abandon the global warming problem and pull the plug on the Kyoto Protocol. (Launched in 1997, this sought to be an undertaking by more than one hundred nations to reduce emissions of the 'greenhouse gases' that cause global warming.) I shall not attempt to provide a detailed analysis of this destructive U-turn; it is sufficient to note that by killing the protocol – in defiance of Europe and many Third World countries – Bush showed the true nature of the globalised American economy. His country was condemned as 'a greedy, selfish, polluting pariah'. It is worth remembering that, although the US has only 4% of the world's population, it produces 25% of greenhouse gases. Britain's Deputy Prime Minister, John Prescott, reacted angrily to Bush's decision, saying that the US 'must know it cannot pollute the world while free-riding on action by everyone else.'[31]

From the point of view of justice theory, it can be argued that Bush's action defies all aspects of justice. However, his decision was not concerned with justice; as he himself observed, it was based on economics, on jobs for Americans and his country's global competitiveness.[32]

There is however a moral issue here. John Prescott pointed out:

All politicians have to live with their consciences, but whether American, European, African or Asian, it is children who have to live with their decisions. We owe it to our children to pass on our planet in better shape than we inherited it.[33]

The above observation endorses my own sentiments about the globalised market economy controlling our lives. The free-market system defends free competition in trade and business but such 'free' competition does not begin with equal possibilities for all the participants. Underlying this system

there is an interpretation of the world and of the human being: a philosophy, a religious perspective, a theology and it is at odds with Catholic justice theory because it dignifies greed, destroys God's earth, has no sense of companionship with the rest of nature, and has no effective concern for the poor.[34]

The Catholic tradition of teaching moral and social justice has meant that many popes, including John Paul II, have expressed great interest in such concerns. The encyclical letter of Pope John Paul II of 1987 on *Social Concern* (*Sollicitudo Rei Socialis*) is indeed one of the most important expressions of the official social doctrine of the Church. He analyses the negative aspects of the actual social situation, saying: 'innumerable multitudes of people suffer an intolerable poverty that has worsened. This is unacceptable in the perspective of Jesus.'[35]

Despite the inspiring power of such encyclical letters, sadly these social teachings, as Fr Munera has so correctly observed, are unknown to the great majority of Catholics worldwide. This anomaly has led many of them to follow, in their moral practice, the religion of the free market and not the religion of Jesus.[36] Nonetheless, following the example set by Pope John Paul II, modern Catholic moral theology seeks increasingly to promote the following of the example of Jesus when guiding the contemporary behaviour of Catholics.

This new theology, born in Latin America where great numbers of Catholics live and work, includes other specificities in its method which have allowed it to assume the name of 'liberation theology'. It proposes that the object of theology is 'praxis'. This, Fr Munera argues, is not simply 'practice', understood as the application of principles to one's own reality; praxis is the commitment of a person to the struggle for liberation from the injustice that oppresses the majority of mankind. In this sense, we can see theology as a critical reflection of praxis in the light of the world.[37] The needs of the poor give perspective to this method. This is in line with the traditional Christian and biblical perspective, for throughout the history of God's self-manifestation the divine predilection for the poor is clearly evident.

Such issues have been the subject of many scholarly works by Catholic theologians.[38] I should like to concentrate in some detail on the work of Fr Munera, who has recently addressed these questions.

As he has so powerfully demonstrated, God chose to become a poor man, Jesus Christ, to preach the Gospel to the poor and to liberate them from injustice and oppression (*Luke* 4: 16-20; citing *Isa.* 61: 1-2). This is why liberation theology teaches first of all that we follow the humble Jesus, assuming his commitment to the liberation of the poor and the oppressed. This means practicing Christianity from the perspective of the poor and oppressed and for their benefit. In Fr Munera's words,

... the stress on praxis in order to transform the situation of injustice by the struggle for liberation is the heart and soul of Catholic liberation theology. Theology must offer solutions to the real problems of the people, specifically a real liberation from the concrete injustices and from any kind of oppression and poverty.

He then refers to the New Testament, specifically to John and Paul, whose conversions show that the following of Christ requires a transformation so fundamental that it is compared to a new birth (*1 Pt.* 2: 2), a new creation, the formation of a new person (*Eph.* 2: 15; 4: 24) who does not have the same characteristics as the old person who is left behind completely (*Rom.* 6: 6). It is like returning to the womb (*John* 3: 1ff), or a definitive passing from darkness to light (*2 Cor.* 4: 6; *Eph.* 5: 8; *1 Pt.* 2: 9), from blindness to vision (*John* 9: 1ff), from silence to word (*Matt.* 9: 33), from leprosy to health (*Matt.* 8: 3), from paralysis to movement (*Matt.* 9: 6), from exile to homecoming (*Luke* 15: 20), from being lost to being found (*Luke* 15: 6), from separation to proximity (*Eph.* 2: 12-13), and from death to life (*Rom.* 6: 13; *John* 5: 34; *John* 3: 14).

In all, according to Fr Munera, the Christian understanding of the world and of the human being, and the experience of being transformed into a replica of Jesus, form the basis of Christian moral conduct and our relationship both with the world and with other people. Practically the whole of the New Testament teaches that the love of others and of the whole cosmos and history is the only commandment, the only norm of morality for human behaviour.[39]

To transform a world of injustice, however, is no easy task. According to Catholic teaching it must begin with the personal determination of a radical change within the most profound interior of the heart, through a conversion to God. And it must involve a commitment to justice. This religious and ontological transformation will lead to a change in attitudes, in systems of life. It will enable just decisions to be made regarding the liberation of the poorest and weakest members of society. This aptly brings us to a closer study of Catholic social teaching in the following section.

4 A Perspective on the Social Teachings of the Catholic Church

THE PURPOSE OF THIS SECTION is to provide an analysis of the social teaching of the Catholic Church, with special emphasis on solidarity, subsidiarity and the common good. As Jürgen Moltmann, in *God for a Secular Society*,[40] has so meaningfully noted, liberation from violence, brutality and poverty remains the central theme of every practical theology and theological praxis; but there is another theme as well as liberty, a theme that has almost been forgotten. This is equality. Equality is a fundamental concern of Catholic justice theory.

Moltmann argues that without equality there is no free world. It is 'self-evident' in the spirit of early Christianity, which we call the truth, that all human beings are created free and equal. Equality does not mean collectivism. It means equal conditions for living and equal chances in life for everyone. As a social concept, equality means justice. As a humanitarian concept, equality means solidarity. As a Christian concept, equality means love.

Moltmann stresses that either we shall create a world of social justice, human solidarity and Christian love or this world will perish through the oppression of people by people, through a social egotism, and through the destruction of the future in the interests of short-term, present-day profits.[41] The Vatican Council of course promotes a social doctrine based on Christian love, justice and solidarity – in other words equality. In the words of Pope John XXIII, 'love is the driving force of the economy', the hallmark of the Christian social doctrine.

My intention is to concentrate on an analysis of the concepts of solidarity, subsidiarity and the common good, and to this theme I now return. One of the most important contributions to the study of Catholic social teaching is by Fr Charles, SJ. This is his *Christian Social Witness and Teaching*[42], to which I shall refer in some detail.

I SOLIDARITY

HUMAN SOCIETY, Fr Charles has argued, needs a principle of unity that goes beyond simple self-interest. Self-interest is important and need not be bad: the love that we have for ourselves is a demonstration of how we should love others. However, sadly this second aspect of it is often forgotten and self-interest can result in the abuse of the rights of others.

The soundest basis for solidarity in human society is the truth that the whole human race is made in God's image, and that all men and women are therefore entitled to be treated with respect and trust. They should be given their rights and they should be expected to accept their responsibilities, as sons and daughters of God.

It is only the transcendent dimension, the belief that there is a power above us to which we are subject by virtue of our natures, which can provide the framework within which common humanity can be expected to accept the restraints on human selfishness required by a healthy society. We cannot avoid our obligation as Christians of keeping this truth before society. However, as Fr Charles importantly reminds us, this is not specifically a Christian insight: it is an insight which the Stoic philosophers had, as have many of the non-Christian religions of the world.

That non-believers and believers who are of this mind often disagree on how they should work in society to see this truth become a reality, does not invalidate the truth in itself. It is a cultural, not a political gift.

The foundations of solidarity must be built on beliefs and traditions that accept the transcendent and make it the measure of human purpose and happiness.[43] *Sollicitudo Rei Socialis* notes that

Today perhaps more than in the past, we realise that human beings are linked by a common destiny which we have to construct together if catastrophe for all is to be avoided. From anguish, fear and escapist phenomena like drugs, the idea emerges that the good to which we are all called and the happiness to which we aspire cannot be obtained without effort and commitment, renouncing personal selfishness.[44]

To achieve solidarity within a society its citizens need to recognise each other as persons. Those who are more influential because they have a greater share of goods and common services should feel a sense of responsibility for the weaker and be ready to share with them all that they possess.

Awareness of our interdependence, a moral and social attitude of solidarity, a firm and persevering commitment to the common good, that is, to the good of all and of each individual, because we are all responsible for all; and readiness to serve – these are better than feelings of vague compassion or shallow distress. This solidarity helps us to see other people not just as instruments to be exploited at low cost but as sharers in the banquet of life to which God invites us all. Solidarity is a Christian virtue of self-giving love.[45]

Finally, as Fr Charles has observed, solidarity is the direct requirement of human and supernatural brotherhood. The serious socio-economic problems that occur today cannot be solved unless new fronts of solidarity are created: solidarity of the poor among themselves, solidarity with the poor to which the rich are called, solidarity among the workers and with the workers. Furthermore, institutions and social organisations at different levels, as well as the state, must share in the general movement of solidarity. When the Church appeals for such solidarity, she is aware that she herself is concerned in quite a special way.[46] *Rerum Novarum* (*Of Revolutionary Change*), issued by Pope Leo XIII in 1891, was the first major document in which the Church confronted the situation in the liberal capitalist industrialised societies of Europe and North America. It is also known as 'The Worker's Charter'.

McOustra, in *Love in the Economy*,[47] has noted that it was revolutionary change that led to this encyclical: the industrial revolution brought economic and social upheaval, complicated by scientific discovery and commercial expansion bringing new wealth and new power. Disfiguring the advances came revolutionary new exploitation and injustice for many. The situation then, it seems, was not dissimilar to our own:

Working men are now left isolated and helpless betrayed by the inhumanity of employers and the unbridled greed of competitors. A tiny group of extravagantly rich men have been able to lay upon a great multitude of unpropertied workers a yoke little better than slavery itself.

Overwhelmingly, Fr Charles has observed, the defects of the system were laid at the door of liberal capitalists and the economic interests they represented. However, according to *Rerum Novarum*, the unpropertied worker also had obligations.

[He] must fulfil faithfully and complete whatever contract of employment he has freely and justly made; do no damage to the property nor harm the person of his employers; to refrain from the use of force in defence of his own interests and inciting civil discord.

For others, *Rerum Novarum* is an indictment of the way in which liberal capitalism, and the states controlled by it, had seriously offended against justice, thus creating the social problem.

The first task is to save workers from the brutality of those who make use of human beings as mere instruments in the creation of wealth, impose a burden of labour which stupefies minds and exhausts bodies. Let workers and employers make bargains freely about wages, but there underlies a requirement of natural justice higher and older than any bargain; a wage ought not to be insufficient for needs.[48]

Solidarity and love are, according to *Rerum Novarum* and *Gaudium et Spes*, the key:

All men have the same Father who is God the creator, the same benefits of nature and gifts of divine grace belonging in common to the whole human race: 'we are children, we are heirs as well; heirs of God and co-heirs with Christ.

The key to success in all these matters is self-giving love.[49]

The fundamental law of human perfection and hence of the transformation of the world is the new commandment of love. The way of love is open to everyone. This love is not something reserved for important matters, but must be exercised above all in the ordinary circumstances of daily life. Despite the infections of evil and sin in the world, despite the crosses we have to carry, Christ with the authority of his resurrection is at work in our hearts by the power of his spirit. Not only does he arouse desire for the world to come but he stimulates, purifies and strengthens our generous and unselfish aspirations to make our present life more human and to bring the earth's resources into the service of this more human life.[50]

Finally, consider what, when Judas Iscariot had gone, Jesus said to his disciples ... (*John* 13: 31, 34-35):

I give you a new Commandment: love one another; you must love one another just as I have loved you. It is by your love for one another, that everyone will recognise you as my disciples.

II SUBSIDIARITY

THE TERM 'SUBSIDIARITY' (from the Latin *subsidium* which means 'help') was used first in the encyclical *Quadragesimo Anno* in 1931. Fr Charles has noted, however, that such an obligation was already indicated in the law of the Old Testament, with its injunctions to succour the widow, the orphan and the stranger in their need. In the New Testament the notion of subsidiarity was highlighted in the parable of the Good Samaritan, and it has been present in the social welfare work of the Church throughout its history. Looking at *Rerum Novarum*, it is clear that it was there also, where the duty of the state to care for the weak and the poor was emphasised. The idea of subsidiarity, according to Fr Charles, sums up the Christian obligation to help others in their need, when unemployment, poverty or serious illness prevents them from supporting themselves. *Quadragesimo Anno* observes:

Much that we cannot accomplish as individuals alone, we can best do by working together in association ... It is an injustice and at the same time a great evil and disturbance of right order to assign to a greater and higher association what lesser and subordinate organisations can do. For every social activity ought of its very nature to furnish help to the members of the body social, and never destroy or absorb them.[51]

Furthermore, according to *Pacem in Terris*,

Recognition of rights, observance of duties, and collaboration with others should be primarily matters of personal decision, each of us acting on our own initiative, conviction, and sense of responsibility. There is nothing human about a society that is welded together by force. Society must be based on truth, and will be, if we each acknowledge our rights and duties. Human society demands justice, love, freedom, and responsibility, and is thus primarily a spiritual reality having its origin in God, the deepest source from which human society can draw genuine vitality. An important requirement upon the state is to ensure fair and favourable conditions for enjoyment of rights and fulfilment of duties by all its citizens in freedom, and for contribution to the common good, material and spiritual, by individuals and groups.[52]

Finally, as Fr Charles has noted, if only solidarity can be built out of a sound metaphysical or theological inheritance properly fostered by the state, subsidiarity is very much the fruit of the right sort of state action. Civil society, according to our Christian understanding, is based on personal moral responsibility, encouraged by the right values and founded on the eternal, revealed and natural laws. It is achieved through a healthy family life that fosters these values. In this way a capable and morally responsible citizenry can develop and groups can co-operate with one another in economic, social and cultural activities. Patterns of associations are developed in the pursuit of common aims and objectives. Finally, a political society emerges for the very purpose of securing the common good, the good of each and the good of all.[53] This is the subject of the final part of this chapter.

III COMMON GOOD

ONE OF THE BEST DEFINITIONS of the common good was given in *Gaudium et Spes* (*The Church in the Modern World*), the Pastoral Constitution of the Second Vatican Council (1965). This is how the concept is defined:

As interdependence grows, so does the point of 'the common good', which is 'the sum total of social conditions which allow people, as groups or as individuals, to reach fulfilment more fully and more easily'. Every group must take into account the needs and aspirations of every other group, and of the whole human family.

At the same time, because of the dignity of the human person, the individual has rights and duties that are universal and inviolable. Every human being should have ready access to everything necessary for living a truly human life, including food, clothes, housing, education, work, respect, and the right to act according to correct conscience.

The social order and its development must yield to the good of the person, since the order of things must be subordinate to the order of persons and not the other way round ...' We must constantly improve the social order, in truth, justice, and love. We should renew our attitudes; change our mentality.

We must have respect for one another, and for our neighbours' needs for a decent quality of life. We must make ourself the neighbour of every person in need whom we can help. Whatever offends human dignity, such as sub-human living conditions, or treatment of employees as mere tools for profit instead of free, responsible men and women: these and the like poisons civilisation.

... No one today should be content to lounge in a merely individual-istic morality. The best way to fulfil our obligations of justice and love is to contribute to the common good, and to promote and help public and private organisations working for better conditions of life.[54]

In *Mater et Magistra* (*Mother and Teacher*, 1961), Pope John XXIII mentions the common good and its relation to business.

We must not consider only the claims of pay and of profit, within busi-ness. We must also consider the common good, at home and abroad. The demands of the common good include employment, for the greatest number; balance between pay and prices; the need to make goods and services accessible to the greatest number; balance between economic expansion and social services; adjustment to the progress of science and technology; the development of less advanced economies;

and the need to make the prosperity of a more human way of life available not only to the present generation but to coming generations as well.

We must also consider the common good when assessing interest, dividends, and rewards to directors.[55]

In *Codex Iuris Canonici* (*The Code of Canon Law*, 1983), in Book III which deals with the teaching office of the Church, the relationship between common good and education is noted:

Education must pay regard to the formation of the whole person, so that all may attain their eternal destiny and at the same time promote the common good of society. Children and young persons are therefore to be cared for in such a way that their physical, moral and intellectual talents may develop in a harmonious manner, so that they may attain a greater sense of responsibility and a right use of freedom, and be formed to take an active part in social life.[56]

In a recent study, *The Natural Economy*, John Young has defined the common good as, 'A non-exclusive benefit, desired as a social end, and achieved through association.'[57] The non-appropriative, or non-restrictive, feature of the common good, according to Young, is its fundamental characteristic. Reflect on friendship, or peace, or knowledge. In each case the same quality is present: the quality of being capable of possession by any number of people without diminution of what each receives. The common good is desired in common by the members of a group: it constitutes the end or object, the *raison d'être*, of the group. Members of the group do not attain it as individuals, only insofar as they are associated with one another. They attain it as a society; they achieve it in common. Each member of the society contributes talents, encouragement and so on, and all the contributions are 'socialised' into a whole, and this whole is more than a collection of the individual parts. Association has within itself a dynamism derived from the individuals, yet transcending them.[58]

The common good is common in three ways:

It is common in its nature (distributiveley as opposed to collectively – is of such a nature that its possession by one does not limit its possession by others); it is common as an end desired (this common end is what makes something be a society and not merely a gathering of individuals); and it is achieved or actualised in common (not by a collection of individual efforts).[59]

Placing these elements in the order of attainment, it is commonly desired, commonly achieved, commonly possessed. It can also be thus defined as 'a good desired in common, achieved in common and possessed in common'.

As Young has argued, an understanding of the common good throws a flood of light on the nature of society, on its unity or lack of it, and on its deviations from the ideal. It shows up what is good in society, and also shows us that the evils with which society is riddled are due to the perversion of the common good, which ought to be able to flourish so much more than it does.[60]

In this chapter I began with an attempt to define the promised land. I argued that the promised land is a land abundant in justice, love, compassion, sympathy, empathy, community, solidarity and the common good, very different from our current wasteland beset by individualism, self-interest, profit-maximisation, greed, godlessness, materialism, unethical behaviour, sleaze and corruption. I then noted that today's free market is not just an economic system but a religion, although not a very good one as it can only thrive by promising a secular salvation that it never supplies. I then argued that any solution to the problems of the free market must have a religious dimension and I tried to provide an analysis of the solutions provided by the Catholic Church, as an example of what traditional religions as a whole have to offer.

Afterword: A Pause for Thought
on Those Bent On Destroying the World
in Pursuit of Greed

RECENTLY GEORGE BUSH published his energy proposal. In it there is little reference to energy conservation and respect for the environment and much emphasis on massive energy production at all costs. Amongst its recommendations are the following:

Recommendation number one: build many nuclear plants. This was a very good deal for the biggest builder of nuclear plants, based in Texas, the Brown & Root subsidiary of the Halliburton Corporation, whose recent chief executive was Vice-President Dick Cheney.

Recommendation number two: drill for oil in Alaska's arctic wildlife refuge. This policy was recommended by Don Evans, Bush's Commerce Secretary. Evans, until recently, was chief executive of Tom Brown Inc, a billion-dollar oil and gas corporation.

Former Texas agriculture commissioner Jim Hightower, commenting on these recommendations, observed, 'They've eliminated the middle man. The corporations don't have to lobby the government anymore. They are the government.' Hightower used to complain about Monsanto lobbying the Secretary of Agriculture. Today, former Monsanto executive Ann Venamin is the Secretary of Agriculture.

Considering the above policy recommendations and Bush's appointments to his cabinet, important questions should be asked: Can one deny that the petro-chemical industry's contribution of $48m to the Republican campaign of 2000 has had any impact on the President's decision? Furthermore, are these contributions, with their resultant consequences, ethical, moral, or good for democracy?

Second Pause for Thought:
A Warning to Those who are Bent on Destroying the World in Pursuit of their Greed

Only when the last tree has died and the last river been poisoned and the last fish been caught will we realise we cannot eat money.[61]

CHAPTER 5

Men like Henry George are rare unfortunately. One cannot imagine a more beautiful combination of intellectual keenness, artistic form, and fervent love of justice.

ALBERT EINSTEIN

Who reads will find in Henry George's philosophy a rare beauty and power of inspiration, and a splendid faith in the essential nobility of human nature.

HELEN KELLER

All the country needs is new and sincere thought, coherently, distinctly and boldly uttered by men who are sure of their ground. The power of men like Henry George seems to me to mean that.

WOODROW WILSON

People do not argue with the teachings of George they simply do not know it … He who becomes acquainted with it cannot but agree.

COUNT LEO TOLSTOY

Landlords grow richer in their sleep without working, risking or economising. The increase in the value of land, arising as it does from the efforts of an entire community, should belong to the community and not to the individual who might hold title.

JOHN STUART MILL

When the missionaries first came, they had the bible and we had the land. Now we have the bible and they have the land.

ARCHBISHOP DESMOND TUTU

Promised Land Revisited: A Philosophy for a Progressive and Just Society

---

I N THE PREVIOUS CHAPTERS I tried to show how destructive certain aspects of neo-classical economics could be. I argued that our current global economy amounts to little more than the privileged few plundering the unprivileged masses, and how, in order to satisfy their greed and their desire to maximise profits and minimise costs, the privileged few have seriously damaged our environment and set in motion dangerous ecological changes. I have also emphasized some of the major global socio-economic crises such as poverty, inequality, injustice, indebtedness, marginalisation, exclusion, isolation, stress, anxiety and depression, as well as secularisation and the removal of God from our daily lives.

So deep is the modern world's economic malaise that, in the words of Hudson *et al*, it needs more than just a clean slate and a fresh start. It needs a philosophy for a fair society.[1] Here, given our concerns, the model I offer to take us to the promised land is the Georgist paradigm, named after the American social reformer and economist, Henry George (1839-97), author of *Progress and Poverty*[2].

I consider that George is a model to be emulated as his economic arguments were reinforced, indeed dominated, by humanitarian and religious philosophy. His forceful criticism of 'privilege', his emphasis on humanity in economics, his demand for equality of opportunity and his systemic economic analysis provide a stimulus to orderly reform.

If you trace out, in the way I have tried to outline, the laws of the production and exchange of wealth, you will see the causes of social

75

weakness and disease in enactments which selfishness has imposed on ignorance, and in maladjustments entirely within our own control. And you will see the remedies. Not in wild dreams of red destruction nor weak projects for putting men in leading strings to a brainless abstraction called the state, but in simple measures sanctioned by justice. You will see in light the great remedy, in freedom the great solvent. You will see that the true law of social life is the law of love, the law of liberty, the law of each for all and all for each; that the golden rule of morals is also the golden rule of the science of wealth; that the highest expressions of religious truth include the widest generalisations of political economy. There will grow on you, as no moralising could teach, a deepening realisation of the brotherhood and sisterhood of humanity; there will come to you a firmer and firmer conviction of the fatherhood of God.[3]

To avert environmental degradation, to eliminate involuntary poverty and unemployment, and to enable each individual to attain his maximum potential, George wrote his extraordinary treatise over 120 years ago. However, at this time of global calamity, his ideas are as valid and relevant today as when he wrote them:

He who makes should have; he who saves should enjoy; what the community produces belongs to the community for communal uses; and God's earth, all of it, is the right of the people who inhabit the earth.

Given the main thrust of my study, which has been to provide solutions to our global socio-economic crises based mainly on Catholic social teachings, I am pleased to report that George's ideas are in harmony with, and show respect for, Catholic social doctrine. As John Young has observed, a major theme in George's economics is the role of human association or co-operation. George emphasises the enormous difference between the poverty-stricken existences people would live in isolation and the abundance which is possible through association. He argues that association, like capital, creates wealth, permitting a division of labour, in addition to all the other advantages arising from a community of people. The term 'solidarity' (see Chapter 4), as used in Catholic social doctrine, has the same meaning as 'association' in George's writings.

At the centre of Georgist thought is the conviction that a human being has dignity: this is essential to the fullest freedom consistent with the common good (another main tenet of Catholic social doctrine). Although he advocated the benefits of competition and free trade, this was within the context of justice, which ensured a fair distribution of wealth, and an ethical approach to trade and competition. George always remembered that the economy is a part of the total social system, and that if it is diseased this will infect other areas of social life.[4]

Looking at George's writings, one can observe his constant concern for humanity and for justice:

For poverty is not merely deprivation, it means shame, degradation; the searing of the most sensitive parts of our moral and mental nature as with hot irons; the denial of the strongest impulses and the sweetest affections; the wrenching of the most vital nerves.[5]

He fundamentally disagrees with those economists who see self-interest as the main driving force of human action:

It is not selfishness that enriches the annals of every people with heroes and saints ... It was not selfishness that turned Gautama's back to his royal home or bade the Maid of Orleans lift the sword from the altar ...[6]

In formulating his philosophy George was much influenced by what he observed in San Francisco in the 1850s, where he had a unique opportunity of studying the formation of a community as he watched it change from an encampment into a thriving metropolis.[7] He saw a city of tents and mud change into a fine town of paved streets and decent housing, with tramways and buses. But as he saw the beginnings of wealth, he noted the first appearance of pauperism. He saw growing degradation at the same time as he saw the advent of leisure and affluence, and he felt compelled to discover why they arose concurrently. He wrote, 'the association of progress with poverty is the great enigma of our times', and this is as true today as it was in 1879.

It is the central fact from which spring industrial, social, and political difficulties that perplex the world, and with which statesmanship and philanthropy and education grapple in vain. From it come the clouds that overhang the future of the most progressive and self-reliant nations. It is the riddle that the sphinx of fate puts to our civilisation, which not to answer is to be destroyed. So long as all the increased wealth which modern progress brings goes but to build up great fortunes, to increase luxury and make sharper the contrast between the House of Have and the House of Want, progress is not real and cannot be permanent.[8]

Broadly speaking, within the Georgist paradigm a society without economic (as well as political) justice is plagued by systemic inefficiencies rooted in ill-managed conflict. In due course, growing inequality arising from institutional mal-adjustments can, and does, bring civilisations down. Equity is necessary for intergenerational efficiency.[9] This can be seen most clearly in past civilisations – Middle Bronze Age Mesopotamia (2000-1600 BC), Classical antiquity (750 BC-AD 300) and the Byzantine Empire (AD 330-1204). These civilisations collapsed as a result of the corrosive dynamics of debt, absentee landownership, monopolisation and economic polarisation. The interaction of these influences has destroyed societies repeatedly throughout history.[10] These factors were most influential in bringing down the 2,500-year-old Persian monarchy, when in 1979 the Pahlavi Dynasty in Iran fell – those particular issues I have addressed elsewhere.[11]

Such historical overviews can provide a basic insight into the nature of today's global economic crises. Henry George well understood historical relevance. He noted that the means of producing wealth could differ radically: sometimes wealth is stolen from the people, sometimes it is honestly earned. He differentiated between the two where others have not. The consequences of our failure to discern this difference underlie our present troubles. Each great civilization has succumbed through such lack of understanding. It is not valid to say that our times are more complex than ages past, therefore the solu-tion must be more complex. The problems are, on the whole, the same. The fact that we now have electricity, computers and mobile phones does not mean that we cannot succumb to the consequences of injustice that toppled other civilisations.[12] It is possible to have another dark age.

However in George there is a voice of hope. What Geor-gists propose amounts to nothing less than a new paradigm of social organisation. In their view, government is the guardian of natural and social resources, which are the common property of all. George himself said it best:

This revenue arising from the common property could be applied to the common benefit, as were the revenues of Sparta ... Government would change its character, and would become the administration of a great co-operative society. It would become merely the agency by which the common property was administered for the common benefit.[13]

In mainstream economics, it has long been traditional to lament the painful 'trade-off' between equity and efficiency. In the Georgist paradigm this problem has been overcome. Gaffney puts the case succinctly:

Georgist policy has been shown as a means to revive dying cities, and in the process to reconcile equity and efficiency, to reconcile economics with taxation, and to reconcile capital formation with taxation of the rich. It can be seen as a means of harmonising collectivism and individualism in the most constructive possible ways.[14]

Another important aspect of Georgist policy, which is very relevant to today's crises, is its harmony with, and respect for, the environment. The current debate can indeed be enriched by Georgist suggestions as to how scarce natural resources may be shared fairly and efficiently. The Georgist paradigm could offer a conceptual framework and an ethical basis for integrating these and other issues of public policy.[15]

As Kris Feder has observed in two recent major studies, the philosophy of Henry George, particularly his mechanism for socialising land rent, offers a workable synthesis of capitalism and socialism which avoids the fatal flaws of each. Our global environmental crisis will no doubt provide the catalyst for this transformation.[16]

The scarcity of natural resources and the problem of pollution make us all realise that land is scarce and valuable. International negotiations to manage the global commons need to solve the problem of the efficient allocation of as-yet-unowned resources, and the equitable distribution of their rents.[17]

As I mentioned earlier, Georgist philosophy is participatory; for it to become successful it must be embraced by all of the people. This is the challenge. There will have to be a powerful demonstration of the collective will for moral regeneration, a determined application of our sense of fairness, and a sensitivity to the needs of the community, rather than a pursuit of narrow self-interest. The Georgist paradigm presupposes general participation in the process of change: this is necessary for a shift towards higher moral values. Rights prescribed in the model entail corresponding duties for the individual. This is not a social transformation from above that can be entrusted to an elite vanguard.[18] Therefore it can be concluded that the Georgist paradigm challenges the main features of the current capitalist model and neo-classical economics, and this can give us hope.

It is the Georgist paradigm of economic efficiency alongside economic equity, the removal of poverty and the respect for ethics, morality and religion, that in my view is needed today, faced as we are with billions of materially and spiritually impoverished people in the First, Second and Third Worlds. This is not a utopian dream. The failure of Communism and capitalism show the tragedy of rootlessness, exclusion and marginalisation that has befallen the people of the world. As we begin a new millennium, let us look back at and learn from the last one.

By the million people have died in the defence of land that did not belong to them, deceived by the ideology of nationalism. By the million they have starved to death for want of access to the soil, while being admonished as slothful. By the million they have wandered the world for the want of homes of their own, refugees in a world that begrudged them space and accused them of being 'bogus' or 'economic migrants'. In the words of Feder and Harrison, if, in the 21st century, there is to be a resolution of the crises that afflict people in their daily lives, it will not be found in an escape into the heavens. Peace and prosperity for everyone will remain beyond our reach until the day we find our way to *a philosophy for a fair society*.[19] Such a philosophy is present in the Georgist paradigm. It is absent from the ideas of neo-classical economics, and politicians selected, appointed, supported by big business to promote the greedy corporate agenda. Railtrack, Marconi and Enron are recent examples of the dangers.

CHAPTER 6

✳

Through interreligious dialogue we are able to bear witness
to those truths which are the necessary points of reference
for the individual and for society: the dignity of each and
every human being, whatever his or her ethnic origin,
religious affiliation, or political commitment.

POPE JOHN PAUL II

Logically and practically, multiplicity now takes priority
over unity ... the multiplicity of religions is not an evil
which needs to be removed, but rather a wealth which is to
be welcomed and enjoyed by all. EDWARD SCHILLEBEECKX

No government or social agency can on its own meet the
enormous challenges of development of our age. Partner-
ships are required across the broad range of society. In
drawing upon its spiritual and communal resources, religion
can be a powerful partner in such causes as meeting the
challenges of poverty, alienation and the abuse of women
and children and the destructive disregard for our natural
environment. NELSON MANDELA

O God
From whom on different paths
All of us have come,
To whom on different paths
All of us are going,
Make strong in our hearts what unites us,
Build bridges across all that divides us,
United makes us rejoice in our diversity
At one in our witness to that peace
Which you, O god, alone can give.

THE SOUL OF EUROPE PRAYER

CHAPTER 6

Common Problems and Crises: Common Front and Common Hope – An Interreligious Perspective

THE EXPERIENCE AND THE PROCESS that have given birth to this book are based on academic enrichment as well as on a profound personal experience and development.

Before beginning my debate and analysis in this chapter, I should like to explain how and why I have become a true believer in an interreligious perspective. The following are some of the experiences which have shaped my current thinking.

Firstly, in my academic career which has spanned over two decades, I have had the privilege of teaching thousands of students from many different parts of the world, representing many diverse historical, cultural and religious traditions. As well as teaching them in the classroom, I have also read their dissertations and theses on many different topics and these reflect their diverse backgrounds. Furthermore, in my capacity as pastoral carer, I have spent many hours listening to their concerns, hopes and ambitions. They have been a great source of learning for me and have been instrumental in shaping my ideas. It may be of interest to the reader to note where my students have come from, to appreciate their diversity. They have come from Britain, Spain, Greece, France, Germany, Finland, the former Soviet Union, Canada, the United States, Mexico, Japan, South Korea, Indonesia, Malaysia, Taiwan, Thailand, Hong Kong, Singapore, Iran, Iraq, Saudi Arabia, Kuwait, Palestine, Israel, Syria, Jordan, South Africa, Kenya, Uganda, Australia and New Zealand.

Secondly, my personal background is relevant. I was born in the early 1950s in Tehran, Iran. Although this is mainly a Muslim country, I was much influenced and inspired by the history, culture and civilisation of Persia as a whole. I had many opportunities to mix and interact on a daily basis with Jews, Baha'is, Christians (mainly Armenians), Zoroastrians (theirs was the main religion of pre-Islamic Persia) and the tribal people. My junior and high school education was at establishments endowed by Zoroastrian foundations. From an early age I learned to appreciate the art and beauty of dialogue; and I learned about mutual respect, where nobody attempted to change anybody, where we were only too happy to share with each other. After completing my high school education at the age of eighteen, I came to England, where I lived for five years before going to Canada. In England I met my wife, who is English. In our happy marriage of nearly twenty-eight years I think dialogue and mutual respect have had an important role to play. In Canada, where I studied for my BA and MA, we learned a lot more about dialogue, including interfaith dialogue, and about sharing, and caring. Canada, a melting pot for many diverse people from all over the world, is an ideal place to learn about these issues. I believe that our time in Canada has had a major positive impact on our lives. After nearly five years in Canada, we returned to Britain so that I could take my PhD at Birmingham University. The last twenty years or so, lived in a multi-cultural, multi-race and multi-faith Britain, have brought further positive influences to our lives.

Thirdly, since completing my PhD in 1986, I have had the pleasure of delivering papers at many international conferences in different parts of the world. Once again, I have benefited from sharing ideas on global issues with many academics, researchers, students, businessmen and concerned citizens.

Having made the above three observations, it would be irresponsible of me to dwell on my 'uniqueness' and to imply that only *I* know of, and suffer for, injustice, poverty and environmental degradation, or to proclaim that only *I* have solutions to global human crises and anxieties. As the pains are shared and the crises are common, others are equally qualified to provide their own answers.

In developing my ideas about an interreligious perspective, as well as being shaped by my own experiences, I have also been inspired by Hans Kung and Jürgen Moltmann's observations. They have said respectively:

There can be no peace among the nations without peace among the religions. There can be no peace among the religions without dialogue between the religions. There can be no dialogue between the religions without research into theological foundations.[1]

Without the religious and cultural dialogue between religious communities, no one will be able to understand anything – no Christian, no Jew, no Muslim, and no Hindu or Buddhist. People who just stay in their own little circles and stew in their own juice become stupefied, because wherever they are they always hear only the same thing, the thing that endorses them. But sooner or later, what is no different will become for the people who are no different a matter of indifference. It is only from the other that we become aware of what we ourselves are, and sure of our identity.[2]

Economically, politically, ideologically, socially, historically, and racially, we – the peoples of the world – are all different. These differences have produced much disunity and this has, to a large extent, prevented us from solving our socio-economic and political problems, both at national and global levels. However, one should not despair. There could be an alternative approach, a new model based on inter-faith co-operation working with our current socio-economic and political model to create a new paradigm. This way we could overcome our differences and achieve a much more beneficial and fruitful kind of global development. Instead of a 'clash of civilisations' there could be harmony. Our different civilisations could be united through their belief in the same God.

If we look at the six great global religions, Judaism, Christianity, Islam, Buddhism, Hinduism and Sikhism, we see that all of them believe that there is one transcendent, ultimate reality, which five of them call God. The Hindu may be prepared to describe it as non-personal, or as a personal God in many forms, female as well as male, but the ultimate belief, like that of the Trinitarian Christian, is that reality is one. As

for Buddhism, experts can point out that Buddhism as prac-
ticed in reality does know 'God', indeed a number of gods
taken over from popular religion (Indian religion for example):
these personified natural forces or divinised Kings and Saints
are called upon for protection and help. A natural dialogue is
possible between the monotheistic prophetic religions and the
different branches of Buddhism (Theravada, Mahayana and
Vajrayana). It is a dialogue that has to concentrate on the
comparison of the concept of God with the basic Buddhist
concepts of Nirvana, Shunjata and Dharmakaya. These are all
terms which the great majority of Buddhists do not understand in a nihilistic way but as a positive reality, and which
can be regarded by Christians as parallel terms for 'absolute'.
They fulfil analogous functions to the concept of God.[3]

When studying these religions further, it becomes clear that
faith always leads to obligation; this is another fundamental
belief of all of these religions. Obligations include a command
to worship or meditate, and a requirement to care for one's
fellow human beings. A belief that we are all responsible for
our neighbours is central to all the world's great religions. We
can see the truth of this observation in the following passages:

- Rabbi Hillel (60BCE-10CE): 'Do not do to others what you
  would not want them to do to you' (Shabbat 31a).
- Jesus of Nazareth: 'Whatever you want people to do to
  you, do also to them' (*Matt* 7: 12; *Luke* 6: 31).
- Islam: 'None of you is a believer as long as he does not
  wish his brother what he wishes himself' (*Forty Hadith of
  an-Nawawi*, 13).
- Buddhism: 'A state which is not pleasant or enjoyable for
  me will also not be so for him, and how can I impose on
  another a state which is not pleasant or enjoyable for me?'
  (*Sam Yutta Nikaya* V, 353, 35-342.2).
- Hinduism: 'One should not behave towards others in a
  way which is unpleasant for oneself: that is the essence of
  morality' (*Mahabharata* XIII 114, 8).[4]

Furthermore, all of these religions believe in an after life that transcends death. Another shared belief is that it is right to persuade people of the truth of eternal values such as love and truth, especially in a secular, materialistic society that is not inclined to take religion seriously.

Believing in the same God can bring us much-needed unity. This unity should give us the necessary strength to overcome destructive divisions, enabling us to move away from anxiety and towards a more purposeful and happy life. The idea of interfaith dialogue is that the world's religions should be at peace with each other, and should co-operate in efforts to achieve peace and harmony among nations as well as providing solutions to common socio-political and environmental problems.

Hans Kung's programme for 'a global ethic' is one such effort to bring different religions together in dialogue, to agree an ethic to preserve the world from devastation. This, according to Moltmann, was the message of the Parliament of the World's Religions which met in Chicago in 1993:

We women and men of various religions and regions of the Earth therefore address all people, religious and non-religious. We wish to express the following convictions which we hold in common.

- We all have a responsibility for a better global order.

- Our involvement for the sake of human rights, freedom, justice, peace, and the preservation of the Earth is absolutely necessary.

- Our different religious and cultural traditions must not prevent our common involvement in opposing all forms of inhumanity and working for greater humaneness.

- The principles expressed in this global ethic can be affirmed by all persons with ethical convictions, whether religiously grounded or not.

- As religious and spiritual persons we base our lives on an Ultimate Reality and draw spiritual power and hope therefrom, in trust, in prayer or meditation, in word or silence. We have a special responsibility for the welfare of all humanity and care for the planet earth. We do not consider ourselves better than other women and men, but we trust that the ancient wisdom of our religions can point the way for the future.[5]

A further area in which the major religions can play a vital role is the ecological crisis facing humanity. Up to now they have had little to say at international conferences on the environment, apart from generalities. Not many 'religious' solutions have been put forward.

This is in contrast to some 'minor' religions. Representatives of the 'primitive' animist religions have disseminated profound wisdom about the cycles and rhythms of the earth. At international conferences on the environment the Mayas of Central America, Africans from the Cameroon and elsewhere, Aborigines from Australia, Maoris from New Zealand and native peoples from Canada and the United States have talked about 'mother earth' and 'grandmother moon', and their harmony with the spirit or Tao of the cosmos.

This ancient wisdom, noted Moltmann, which deals with the earth as an organism is certainly pre-industrial, but in a post-industrial age it is going to become highly relevant. Today major religions, as well as striving for world peace, must attempt to become 'religions of the earth', with a sympathetic understanding, if the organism of the earth is to survive, and we with it.[6] This is where dialogue is necessary, where it can play a life-saving role.

As Whaling has observed, just as the dialogue with the rediscovered Aristotle enabled Aquinas to deepen his theological understanding and recast Christian theology for medieval times, so too can the dialogue with Hindus, Buddhists, Muslims and Jews of different parts of the world enable us to understand more and to recast theological ideas to suit the modern situation.[7] Paul F. Knitter in *One Earth, Many Religions* advocates a 'globally responsible' dialogue between the various religious traditions for a universal 'eco-human well-being'. Human liberation, and the well-being of creation today, requires the shared commitment of members of all religious traditions. Social injustice and ecological abuse are intertwined: they must be overcome together; and they can be overcome only through a 'globally responsible, correlational dialogue of religions' capable of transcending differences in a common cause.[8]

The truth of this observation can be seen in the Asian experience. The Thirteenth Annual Meeting of the Indian Theological Association in 1989, under the heading

'Liberative Praxis and Theology of Religious Pluralism', noted that:

In a situation of imposed poverty of the masses and of pluralism of religions and humanist ideologies, the combined struggles of the peoples of different faiths and ideologies for liberation, especially those of the awakened poor and marginalized, become the significant *locus theologicus*, a term of reference for a theology of religions from a liberative perspective ... Underlying [the] pluralism of liberation experiences, there is an implicit transformative understanding of religions. Such an understanding seems to be operative in all critical inter-human and inter-religious action and struggles for liberation ... We are, thereby, called to a re-reading and re-articulating of the fundamental faith-affirmations for a liberating inter-human and inter-religious fellowship of peoples. In this hermeneutic, liberation is understood in terms of a wholeness of humans, nature, cosmos and the Ultimate. In a world divided between the powerful and the powerless, wholeness of liberation always includes a preferential option for the powerless and marginalized.[9]

Finally, as Jacques Dupuis, SJ has so effectively observed, whatever questions remain as to the limits of mutual assimilation and 'cross-fertilization' between religious and theological traditions, one thing seems clear, and it is this:

... harmony between religious communities will not be served by a 'universal theology' which would claim to bypass differences and contradictions: it will be served by the development in the various traditions of theologies which, taking religious pluralism seriously, will assume their mutual differences and resolve to interact in dialogue and cooperation.[10]

Furthermore, for this model and this school of thought to succeed, the role of the individual is of paramount importance. As Moltmann[11] has wisely noted, our conditions won't change unless people change. People must be different if the world is to be different. If we want peace on earth, we must become peaceable men and women. If we want a future for our children and our children's children, we ourselves must overcome our lethargy and our egoism and be born again to a living hope for the future. If life is to survive, and if its deadly enemies are to be defeated, faith must be awakened in us and other people, a 'faith that moves mountains'. The unconditional love for life must awaken in us. There is no future without hope. There is no life without love. There is no new assurance without faith.

In conclusion, in this book I have argued that today, at the dawn of the third millennium, the globalised world economy, despite many significant achievements of the last few decades in areas such as science, technology, medicine, transportation and communication, is facing catastrophic socio-economic, political, cultural and environmental crises.

The great majority of us, all over the world, face problems of inequality, injustice, poverty, greed, marginalisation, exclusion, intolerance, fear, mistrust, xenophobia, sleaze, corruption and ecological ruin. These are the ingredients of wasteland, the land in which we currently live.

From my own academic and professional experience I then argued that economics, and the way it is being taught at our universities worldwide, bears a major responsibility for the existence and persistence of these crises. I pointed out that modern neo-classical economics has major shortcomings: it concentrates almost totally on self-interest, and praises individualism and greed; it has little respect for, or understanding of, the true human values of community, solidarity, common good, morality, ethics and justice. I also argued that modern economics has deprived us of knowing God and of appreciating the important role that religion can play in our everyday economic, political and cultural lives. It is my belief that modern neo-classical economics has been the vehicle in which we have travelled to the current wasteland.

I then attempted to define the promised land, the alternative to the wasteland. It is a land abundant in justice, love, compassion, sympathy, empathy, community, solidarity and respect for the common good, in addition to material prosperity. I noted that today's free market is not just an economic system but a religion, although not a very good one, for it can only thrive by promising a secular salvation that it can never supply. I then argued that any solution to the problems of the free market must also have a religious dimension. Given this, an attempt was made to provide an analysis of the solutions provided by the Catholic Church in its social teachings, as an example of what traditional religions as a whole have to offer.

Later in the book we revisited the promised land, where I attempted to provide a philosophy for a progressive and just society. In order to travel from our wasteland to the promised land, I introduced Henry George's *Progress and Poverty* as our chosen model. I argued that George is worthy of being emulated as his economic arguments are reinforced and dominated by humanitarian and religious considerations. His forceful emphasis on humanity in economics, his demand for equality of opportunity and his systemic economic analysis provide a stimulus to orderly reform. This philosophy is expressed in the Georgist paradigm, but is absent from the free-market economy, free trade and globalisation advocated by neo-classical economics.

In conclusion I argued that, given today's globalisation, we all face common crises and anxieties. Therefore, as the pain is felt by us all, as these crises are a common factor, we are all able to participate in providing solutions. An inter-faith approach, a dialogue to form a common front and provide common hope, is in my view necessary for us to overcome our common problems.

Finally, I would like to appeal to my fellow economists, whether engaged in teaching or research, to grasp the nettle and explore the relevance of ethics, morality and faith to the functioning of the market economy, free trade and globalisation. This is too important an area to exclude. We cannot change the world for the better as long as our subject is trapped within the narrow confines of individualism, self interest and greed, of profit-maximisation and cost-minimisation – an 'each man for himself and the devil take the hindermost' attitude.

If we are to be worthy of the toast given by Lord Keynes shortly before his death in 1946 to 'The Royal Economic Society, economics and economists who are the trustees, not of civilisation, but of the possibility of civilisation',[12] we need to take account of broader issues. We ought to be teaching our students to consider what is good for the community and society, what is for the common good. We should all recognise that the individual is part of the community and the environment, benefiting from both and owing something in return.

The individual has no right to consider only his or her narrow self-interest: a duty is owed to other people and to the environment which supports us all.

My plea is for mainstream economics scholars to build these considerations into their analysis and discover how globalisation can benefit all of humanity, so that economics need no longer hang its head in shame, despised as the 'dismal science'. On the contrary, economics could and should be regarded as a holistic, co-operative and caring subject. It is for us, the economists, to prove that this can be the case.

Notes

Page v

1. R.H. Tawney, *Religion and the Rise of Capitalism*, John Murray, London, 1926.

2. Henry George, quoted by John Stewart in *Standing for Justice: A Biography of Andrew MacLaren MP*, Shepheard-Walwyn, London, 2001.

CHAPTER 1

1. Ulrich Duchrow, *Alternatives to Global Capitalism: Drawn from Biblical History, Designed for Political Action*, International Books with Kairos Europa, Utrecht, The Netherlands, 1998.

2. Indonesian writer Y.B. Mangunwijaya, 16th July 1998, as quoted by Naomi Klein in *No Logo*, HarperCollins, London, 2001.

3. Will Hutton & Anthony Giddens, *On the Edge: Living with Global Capitalism*, Jonathan Cape, London, 2000, pp.vii-xi.

4. As quoted in Anthony Wright, *R.H. Tawney*, Manchester University Press, Manchester, 1987.

5. George Bull, 'Morals and Morality', in *International Minds*, Vol. 10, No. 1, 2000, pp.29-30.

6. See 'The Puzzling Failure of Economics', *The Economist*, 23rd August 1997, p.11.

7. For an excellent study on issues raised here see Amartya Sen, *On Ethics and Economics*, Basil Blackwell, Oxford, 1998, and Paul Ormerod, *The Death of Economics*, Faber & Faber, London, 1994.

8. Paul Ormerod, *op. cit.*, p.205.

9. See Amartya Sen, *op. cit.*, p.2, and Paul Ormerod, *op. cit.*, pp.12-13.

10. John Young, *The Natural Economy*, Shepheard-Walwyn, London, 1996, pp.x-xi.

11. See *ibid*, p.15.

12. For an excellent study of 'brands', their origin, development, function and consequences, see Naomi Klein, *op. cit.*

13. Madeleine Bunting, 'Once They Wanted to Help Others, Now They Want to be Britney Spears', in 'The Common Good', *The Guardian*, 21st March, 2001.

14. Brian Griffiths, *Morality and the Market Place: Christian Alternatives to Capitalism and Socialism*, Hodder & Stoughton, London, 1982, p.29.

15. Ulrich Duchrow, Martin Conway, Bob Goudzwaard & AnnCatherin Jarl, *Next Steps towards a Comprehensive Jubilee: An Invitation to Churches and Ecumenical Groups in Western Europe*, World Council of Churches/World Alliance of Reformed Churches/Kairos Europa, Heidelberg, April 2001. I am grateful to Prof. Duchrow for providing me with a copy of this paper, before its publication.

16. *Ibid*, for evidence on these questions.

17. On the subject of interreligious dialogue, see Pope John Paul II who has recently demonstrated his total support, best expressed in his Apostolic Letter to the Bishops, Clergy and Lay Faithful entitled *Novo Millennio Inuente* (*At the Start of the New Millennium*), which was signed in St Peter's Square on 6th January 2001. In the fourth and final section of this letter, entitled 'Witness to Love', Pope John Paul II writes positively and strongly on the subject of interreligious dialogue. For a commentary and the actual text see *Westminster Interfaith Newsletter*, January 2001, pp.1-3. Other sources are: Austin Flannery, OP (ed), 'The Basic Sixteen Documents', in *Vatican Council II, Constitutions, Decrees, Declarations*, Costello Publishing Company, Northport, NY, April 1996; Jacques Dupuis, SJ, *Toward a Christian Theology of Religious Pluralism*, Orbis Books, Maryknoll, NY, 1997; J. Imbach, *Three Faces of Jesus: How Jews, Christians and Muslims see Him*, Templegate Publishers, Springfield, Ill, 1992; His Holiness the Dalai Lama, *The Good Heart*, Rider, London, 1996; Hans Kung, 'The World Religions in God's Plan of Salvation', in J. Neuner (ed), *Christian Revelation and World Religions*, Burns & Oates, London, 1967; Hans Kung et al., *Christianity and World Religions: Paths of Dialogue with Islam, Hinduism, and Buddhism*, Orbis Books, Maryknoll, NY, 1993; Hans Kung & Karel-Josef Kuschel (eds), *A Global Ethic: The Declaration of the Parliament of the World's Religions*, SCM Press, London, 1993; Karl-Josef Kuschel, *Abraham: A Symbol of Hope for Jews, Christians and Muslims*, SCM Press, London, 1995; John Hick & Paul F. Knitter (eds), *The Myth of Christian Uniqueness: Toward a Pluralistic Theology of Religions*, Orbis Books, Maryknoll, NY, 1987; Harold Coward, *Pluralism in the World Religions*, One World, Oxford, 2000; Kenneth Cragg, *Jesus and the Muslims: An Exploration*, George Allen & Unwin, London, 1985; Jürgen Moltmann, *God for a Secular Society: The Public Relevance of Theology*, SCM Press, London, 1999; Mary Pat Fisher, *Living Religions*, I.B. Tauris, London, 1997; Peter Beyer, *Religion and Globalisation*, Sage Publications, London, 1994; Paul Knitter, *No Other Name? A Critical Survey of Christian Attitudes toward World Religions*, Orbis Books, Maryknoll, NY, 1985; Paul Knitter, *One Earth, Many Religions: Multifaith Dialogue and Global Responsibility*, Orbis Books, Maryknoll, NY, 1995; Ninian Smart, *Dimensions of the Sacred: An Anatomy of the World's Beliefs*, HarperCollins, London, 1996; and Kate M. Loewenthal, *The Psychology of Religion*, One World, Oxford, 2000.

CHAPTER 2

1. Mason Gaffney, Professor of Economics, University of California (Riverside) on how economics is being taught at universities. Quoted in Fred Harrison, *The Corruption of Economics*, Shepheard-Walwyn, London, 1994.

2. Paul Ormerod, former Director of Economics at the Henley Centre for Forecasting, former Head of Economic Assessment Unit (EAU) at *The Economist* and author of *The Death of Economics*, Faber & Faber, London, 1994.

3. Fred Harrison, 'From Chaos to Cosmos', in *The Corruption of Economics*, Shepheard-Walwyn, London, 1994.

4. Amartya Sen, *On Ethics and Economics*, Basil Blackwell, Oxford, 1998.

5. Andrew MacLaren, MP, *Hansard*, 24th February 1937.

6. R.H. Tawney, quoted in Anthony Wright, *R.H. Tawney*, Manchester University Press, Manchester, 1987, p.19.

7. Amartya Sen, *op. cit.*; Mason Gaffney & Fred Harrison, *The Corruption of Economics*, Shepheard-Walwyn, London, in association with Centre for Incentive Taxation Ltd, 1994; and Paul Ormerod, *op. cit.*

8. See Ulrich Duchrow, *Alternatives to Global Capitalism: Drawn from Biblical History, Designed for Political Action*, International Books with Kairos Europa, Utrecht, The Netherlands, 1998; Harold Coward & Daniel C. Maguire (eds), *Visions of a New Earth: Religious Perspectives on Population, Consumption, and Ecology*, State University of New York Press, Albany, NY, 2000; John Young, *The Natural Economy*, Shepheard-Walwyn, London, 1996; Michael Hudson, G.J. Miller & Kris Feder, *A Philosophy for a Fair Society*, Shepheard-Walwyn, London, 1994; E.F. Schumacher, *Small is Beautiful: Economics as if People Mattered*, Blond & Briggs, London, 1973, and *A Guide for the Perplexed*, Jonathan Cape, London, 1977; Robert Andelson & James Dawsey, *From Wasteland to Promised Land: Liberation Theology for a Post-Marxist World*, Orbis Books, Maryknoll, NY and Shepheard-Walwyn, London, 1992; Susan George, *How the Other Half Dies*, Penguin Books, New York, 1976; Henry George, *Progress and Poverty*, 1879, reprinted by Robert Schalkenbach Foundation, New York, 1971; George Ann Potter, *Deeper than Debt: Economic Globalisation and the Poor*, The Latin American Bureau, London, 1999; Gerard Elfstrom, *Moral Issues and Multinational Corporations*, Macmillan, London, and St Martin's Press, New York, 1991; Ruben Alves, *A Theology of Human Hope*, Abbey Press, St Meinrad, Ind, 1975; Reinhold Niebuhr, *Moral Man and Immoral Society*, Scribners, New York, 1932; David Richards, 'Missing Links in the New Economics', *Land and Liberty*, March-April 1987; Christopher McOustra, *Love in the Economy: Social Doctrine of the Church for the Individual in the Economy*, St Paul Publications, Slough, UK, 1990; and Rodger Charles, SJ, *An Introduction to Catholic Social Teaching*, Family Publications, Oxford, 1999.

9. On these issues see Kevin Danaher, 'Power to the People', in *The Observer*, 29th April 2001; and for evidence on this statement see Paul Ormerod, *op. cit.*, p.viii.

10. Singer, Peter (ed), *Blackwell Companions to Philosophy: A Companion to Ethics*, Blackwells, Oxford, 1990.

11. Daniel Maguire in Harold Coward & Daniel Maguire, *op. cit.*, p.1.

12. This section was heavily relied on: *ibid*, pp.1-2.

13. See Amartya Sen, *op. cit.*, pp.ix-xiii, 1-3.

14. See Robert Solomon, 'Business ethics', in Peter Singer, *op. cit.*, pp.354-65, and 'Notes on Calvin, John', in *Electric Library Encyclopedia.com*.

15. For further reading and the evidence for sources used see Amartya Sen, *op. cit.*, pp.1-3.

16. See Paul Ormerod, *op. cit.*, pp.12-13.

17. *Ibid*, pp.12-14.

18. For the full text see Kathryn Sutherland (ed), *An Inquiry Into the Nature and Causes of the Wealth of Nations*, Oxford University Press, Oxford, revised edition 1998.

19. Paul Ormerod, *op. cit.*, p.12.

20. See *Ibid*, p.13.

21. See *ibid*, pp.13-14.

22. See Amartya Sen, *op. cit.*, pp.2-7.

23. *Ibid*, p.4.

24. On the issues raised see Paul Ormerod, *op. cit.*, pp.39-40.

25. See Kathryn Sutherland (ed), *op. cit.*

26. For evidence on this statement and other issues raised see Paul Ormerod, *op. cit.*, p.42.

27. See *ibid*, p.43.

28. *Ibid*.

29. *Ibid*, pp.45-6.

30. See Mason Gaffney & Fred Harrison, *op. cit.*, pp.128-30.

31. *Ibid*, pp.130-1.

32. See Michael Hudson, G.J. Miller & Kris Feder, *op. cit.*, p.155.

33. See Mason Gaffney & Fred Harrison, *op. cit.*, pp.133-4.

34. *Ibid*, p.134.

35. Will Hutton, 'Titanic greed of the telecom giants', in *The Observer*, 22nd April 2001, p.28.

36. *Ibid*.

37. Richard Ingrams, 'One law for Railtrack ...', in *The Observer*, 20th May 2001.

CHAPTER 3

1. Henry George, *Progress and Poverty*, 1879, reprinted by Robert Schalkenbach Foundation, New York, 1971.

2. Felicity Lawrence, 'Mass Affluents Get Richer', in *The Guardian*, 2nd April 2001.

3. Will Hutton, 'The Rich Aren't Cleverer, Just Richer', in *The Observer*, 1st April 2001.

4. Adapted from Naomi Klein, *No Logo*, HarperCollins, London, 2001, p.474.

5. On these issues see Robert Andelson & James Dawsey, *From Wasteland to Promised Land: Liberation Theology for a Post-Marxist World*, Shepheard-Walwyn, London, and Orbis Books, Maryknoll, NY, 1992, pp.1-10.

6. See Michael Hudson, G.J. Miller & Kris Feder, *A Philosophy for A Fair Society*, Shepheard-Walwyn, London, in association with Centre for Incentive Taxation Ltd, 1994, pp.1-31.

7. Mason Gaffney & Fred Harrison, *The Corruption of Economics*, Shepheard-Walwyn, London, in association with Centre for Incentive Taxation Ltd, 1994, p.31.

8. Adapted from George Ann Potter, *Deeper Than Debt: Economic Globalisation and the Poor*, The Latin American Bureau, London, 2000, pp.4-5.

9. See Nigel Dower, 'World Poverty', in Peter Singer (ed), *Blackwell Companions to Philosophy: A Companion to Ethics*, Blackwells, Oxford, 1990, p.273.

10. See Ulrich Duchrow, *Alternatives to Global Capitalism: Drawn from Biblical History, Designed for Political Action*, International Books with Kairos Europa, Utrecht, The Netherlands, 1998, pp.11-17.

11. George Ann Potter, *op. cit.*

12. Kevin Watkins, *Globalisation and Liberalisation: Implications for Poverty, Distribution and Inequality*, UNDP, New York, 1997.

13. On these issues see George Ann Potter, *op. cit.*, pp.4-5; and Ulrich Duchrow, *op. cit.*, p.11.

14. See Ulrich Duchrow, *op. cit.*, pp.11-17.

15. See Oscar Ugarteche in George Ann Potter, *op. cit.*, pp.xi-xiii.

16. On the issues raised so far see George Ann Potter, *op. cit.*, pp.1-7.

17. *Ibid*, p.6.

18. Kamran Mofid, *Development Planning in Iran: From Monarchy to Islamic Republic*, Middle East and North African Studies Press, Wisbech, UK, 1987; and *The Economic Consequences of the Gulf War*, Routledge, London, 1990.

19. See Catherine Howarth *et al.*, 'Monitoring Poverty and Social Exclusion: Labour's Inheritance', in *Joseph Rowntree Foundation*, December 1998; and 'Households Below Average Income (HBA) 1979-1996/7', in *Department of Social Security 1998*.

CHAPTER 4

1. Herman E. Daly & John B. Cobb Jr, *For the Common Good*, Beacon Press, Boston, 1994.

2. R.H. Tawney, Tawney to Mansbridge, 19th March 1909, Rewley House Collection.

3. David R. Loy, 'The Religion of the Market', in Harold Coward & Daniel Maguire (eds), *Visions of a New Earth: Religious Perspectives on Population, Consumption, and Ecology*, State University of New York Press, Albany, NY, 2000.

4. Robert Andelson & James Dawsey, *From Wastland to Promised Land: Liberation Theology for a Post-Marxist World*, Shepheard-Walwyn, London, and Orbis Books, Maryknoll, NY, 1992, pp.1-11, 17-27.

5. See *ibid*, p.24.

6. See *ibid*.

7. *Ibid*, for evidence on this statement.

8. *Ibid*, p.25.

9. *Quadragesimo Anno* (1931), articles 57-8, in *Seven Great Encyclicals*, Paulist Press, Glen Rock, NJ, 1963; quoted by Robert Andelson & James Dawsey, *op. cit.*, p.25.

10. *Quadragesimo Anno* (1931), articles 56-61, 88, 97-8, 105-20, 130-7, in Christopher McOustra, *Love in the Economy: Social Doctrine of the Church for the Individuals in the Economy*, St Paul Publications, Slough, UK, 1990, p.46.

11. *Sollicitudo Rei Socialis* (1987), article 46, in *ibid,* p.171.

12. David Loy, *op. cit.*, pp.15-29.

13. Rodney Dobell, 'Environmental Degradation and the Religion of the Market', in Harold Coward (ed), *Population, Consumption, and the Environment*, State University of New York Press, Albany, NY, 1995; quoted by David Loy, *op. cit.*, pp.16-17.

14. On these issues see *ibid*, pp.16-18.

15. On this and other issues raised see *ibid*, pp.17-19.

16. Karl Polanyi, *The Great Transformation*, Beacon Press, Boston, 1957; quoted by David Loy, *op. cit.*, p.20.

17. See *ibid*.

18. *Ibid.*

19. See *ibid*, pp.24-5.

20. Herman Daly & John Cobb Jr, *op. cit.*; quoted *ibid*, p.26.

21. See *ibid*.

22. For evidence see *ibid*.

23. *Ibid.* pp.26-7.

24. On different religions, and their teachings and solutions to current economic and ecological problems, see the highly recommended book by Harold Coward & Daniel Maguire (eds), *op. cit.*

25. David Loy, *op. cit.*, p.27.

26. Alberto Munera, SJ, 'New Theology on Population, Ecology, and Overconsumption from the Catholic Perspective', 2000, in Harold Coward & Daniel Maguire (eds), *op. cit.*, pp.65-78.

27. See *ibid*, pp.65-7.

28. *Ibid*, p.66.

29. *Ibid*, p.68.

30. *Ibid.*

31. For further reading on these issues see Ed Vulliamy, 'The President Who Bought Power and Sold the World', in *The Observer*, 1st April 2001. For an assessment of Bush's decision on the environment and the people see Robin McKie & Priscilla Morris, 'The World in 2050', in *ibid.*

32. See *ibid.*

33. John Prescott, MP, 'Children Pay for Political Errors', in *ibid.*

34. Alberto Munera, *op. cit.*, p.69.

35. See *Sollicitudo Rei Socialis* (1987), *op. cit.*

36. See Alberto Munera, *op. cit.*, pp.72-4.

37. *Ibid.*

38. See for example: Emil Brunner, *Justice and the Social Order*, Butterworth, London, 1945; Henry Davis, SJ, *Moral and Pastoral Theology*, Vol. 1, Sheed & Ward, London & New York, 1949; Gustavo Gutierrez, *A Theology of Liberation*, Orbis Press, Maryknoll, NY, 1973; Daniel Maguire, 'Catholicism and Modernity', in *Horizons*, 13.2, 1986; I. Ellacurai & John Sabrino, *Mysterium Liberationis: Fundamental Concepts of Liberation Theology*, Orbis Press, Maryknoll, NY, 1993; Jürgen Moltmann, *God for a Secular Society: The Public Relevance of Theology*, SCM Press, London, 1999; John XXIII, *Mater et Magistra*, 15th May 1961; John Paul II, *Sollicitudo Rei Socialis*, *op. cit.*; and Vatican Council II, *Gaudium et Spes*, 1965.

39. See Alberto Munera, SJ, *op. cit.*, pp.74-5. I am much indebted to his highly recommended article, which presents a detailed analysis of Catholic moral justice theory, and its interactions with economics, globalisation, the marketplace and ecology.

40. See Jürgen Moltmann, *op. cit.*, p.69.

41. *Ibid.*

42. Rodger Charles, SJ, *Christian Social Witness and Teaching: The Catholic Tradition from Genesis to Centesimus Annus* (2 vols), Gracewing, Leominster, 1998; and *An Introduction to Catholic Social Teaching*, Family Publication, Oxford, 1999.

43. See *An Introduction to Catholic Social Teaching*, pp.25-6.

44. *Sollicitudo Rei Socialis* (1987), article 26, *op. cit.*

45. *Ibid,* articles 38-40.

46. See *Libertatis Conscientia* (1986), article 89: quoted by Rodger Charles, SJ, *op. cit.*, p.26.

47. See Christopher McOustra, *op. cit.*, p.35.

48. *Rerum Novarum* (1891), articles 2, 17, 43, 45, in Christopher McOustra, *op. cit.*, pp.35-40; and Rodger Charles, SJ, *op. cit.*, pp.33-4.

49. *Ibid.*

50. *Gaudium et Spes* (1969), articles 37, 38, 39, (22), in Christopher McOustra, *op. cit.*, pp.66-81.

51. *Quadragesimo Anno* (1931), articles 78-80, *op. cit.*; and Rodger Charles, SJ, *op. cit.*, pp.35-6.

52. *Pacem in Terris* (1963), articles 34-8, 48, 60, 48-65, in Christopher McOustra, *op. cit.*, pp.61-5.

53. See Rodger Charles, SJ, *op. cit.*, pp.41-3.

54. *Gaudium et Spes* (1965), *op. cit.*, articles 26 (63, 86b), 27 (66), 30.

55. *Mater et Magistra* (1961), articles 78-81, in Christopher McOustra, *op. cit.*, pp.48-59.

56. *Codex Iuris Canonici* (c.795), in Christopher McOustra, *op. cit.*, pp.155-160.

57. John Young, *The Natural Economy*, Shepheard-Walwyn, London, 1996, p.8.

58. See *ibid*, p.9.

59. *Ibid.*

60. *Ibid*, pp.10-15.

61. Quoted in *New Internationalist*, different issues, 2001.

CHAPTER 5

1. See Michael Hudson, G.J. Miller & Kris Feder (hereafter Hudson *et al.*), *A Philosophy for a Fair Society*, Shepheard-Walwyn, London, 1994, p.23.

2. Henry George, *Progress and Poverty*, 1879, reprinted by Robert Schalkenbach Foundation, New York, 1971.

3. Henry George, *op. cit.*, as quoted in *Economic Monitor*, Spring 2001, Issue 73.

4. John Young, 'Was Henry George Right?', in *Social Justice Review*, September/October 1994, pp.153-6.

5. For evidence on this statement see *ibid*, p.153.

6. *Ibid.*

7. For further reading on George's life see Agnes George de Mille, *Who Was Henry George?*, Robert Schalkenbach Foundation, New York, 1979.

8. Henry George, *op. cit.*, Ch 1.

9. See Hudson *et al.*, *op. cit.*, p.155.

10. On these issues see *ibid*, pp.33-80.

11. Kamran Mofid, *Development Planning in Iran: From Monarchy to Islamic Republic*, Middle East and North African Studies (MENAS) Press, Wisbech, UK, 1987.

12. See Agnes George de Mille, *op. cit.*

13. Henry George, *op. cit.*, pp.456-7.

14. Mason Gaffney, 'The Role of Ground Rent in Urban Decay and Revival', as quoted by Hudson *et al.*, *op. cit.*, p.156.

15. See *ibid*, p.157.

16. Richard Noyes (ed), *Now the Synthesis: Capitalism, Socialism, and the New Social Contract*, Shepheard-Walwyn, London, and Holmes & Meier, New York, 1991; and Robert Andelson (ed), *Commons Without Tragedy: The Social Ecology of Land Tenure*, Shepheard-Walwyn, London, and Barnes & Noble, Savage, Maryland, 1991, as quoted by Hudson *et al.*, *op. cit.*, p.157.

17. See *ibid*, p.157.

18. On these issues see Mason Gaffney & Fred Harrison, *The Corruption of Economics*, Shepheard-Walwyn, London, in association with Centre for Incentive Taxation Ltd, 1994, pp.210-15.

19. See Hudson *et al.*, *op. cit.*, pp.219-27.

CHAPTER 6

1. Hans Kung, *Theology for the Third Millennium*, Doubleday, New York, 1988; and *Global Responsibility: In Search of a New World Ethics*, SCM Press, London, 1991, p.105.

2. Jürgen Moltmann, *God for a Secular Society: The Public Relevance of Theology*, SCM Press, London, 1999, pp.227-8.

3. On these issues see W. Owen Cole, *Six Religions in the Twentieth Century*, Stanley Thornes (Publishers), Cheltenham, 1984; and Hans Kung & Karl-Josef Kuschel (eds), *A Global Ethic: The Declaration of the Parliament of the World's Religions*, SCM Press, London, 1993.

4. For evidence on these statements see Hans Kung & Karl-Josef Kuschel (eds), *op. cit.,* pp.71-2.

5. See Jürgen Moltmann, *op. cit.*, p.237 and *ibid,* pp.18-19.

6. On these issues see Jürgen Moltmann, *op. cit.,* pp.237-8.

7. Frank Whaling, *Christian Theology and World Religions: A Global Approach*, Marshall Pickering, London, 1986; as quoted by Jacques Dupuis, SJ, *Toward a Christian Theology of Religious Pluralism*, Orbis Books, Maryknoll, NY, 1997, p.383.

8. Paul Knitter, *One Earth, Many Religions: Multifaith Dialogue and Global Responsibility*, Orbis Books, Maryknoll, NY, 1995; as quoted by Jacques Dupuis, SJ, *op. cit.,* p.377.

9. For evidence see *ibid,* pp.375-6.

10. *Ibid,* p.384.

11. Jürgen Moltmann, *op. cit.,* p.224.

12. Roy Harrod, as quoted in Ronald Burgess, *Public Revenue without Taxation*, Shepheard-Walwyn, London, 1993, p.1.

Bibliography

Alves, Ruben, *A Theology of Human Hope*, Abbey Press, St Meinrad, Ind, 1975.

Andelson, Robert (ed), *Commons Without Tragedy: Protecting the Environment from Overpopulation*, Shepheard-Walwyn, London and Barnes & Noble, Savage, Maryland, 1991.

Andelson, Robert & James Dawsey, *From Wasteland to Promised Land: Liberation Theology for a Post-Marxist World*, Shepheard-Walwyn, London and Orbis Books, Maryknoll, NY, 1992.

Beyer, Peter, *Religion and Globalisation*, Sage Publications, London, 1994.

Brunner, Emil, *Justice and the Social Order*, Butterworth, London, 1945.

Bull, George, 'Morals and Morality', in *International Minds*, Vol. 10, No. 1, 2000.

Bunting, Madeleine, 'Once They Wanted to Help Others, Now They Want to be Britney Spears', in 'The Common Good', *The Guardian*, 21st March 2001.

Charles, Rodger, SJ, *Christian Social Witness and Teaching: The Catholic Tradition from Genesis to Centesimus Annus* (2 vols), Gracewing, Leominster, 1998.

— *An Introduction to Catholic Social Teaching*, Family Publication, Oxford, 1999.

Codex Iuris Canonici (*The Code of Canon Law*), Collins, Glasgow, 1983.

Cole, W. Owen, *Six Religions in the Twentieth Century*, Stanley Thornes (Publishers), Cheltenham, 1984.

Coward, Harold (ed), *Population, Consumption, and the Environment*, State University of New York, Albany, NY, 1995.

— *Pluralism in the World Religions*, One World, Oxford, 2000.

Coward, Harold & Daniel Maguire (eds), *Vision of a New Earth: Religious Perspectives on Population, Consumption and Ecology*, State University of New York, Albany, NY, 2000.

Cragg, Kenneth, *Jesus and the Muslims: An Exploration*, George Allen & Unwin, London, 1985.

Dalai Lama, His Holiness the, *The Good Heart*, Rider, London, 1996.

Daly, Herman E. & John B. Cobb Jr, *For the Common Good*, Beacon Press, Boston, 1994.

Danaher, Kevin, 'Power to the People', *The Observer*, 29th April 2001.

Davis, Henry, SJ, *Moral and Pastoral Theology* (Vol 1), Sheed & Ward, London & New York, 1949.

Department of Social Security, 'Households Below Average Income (HBA), 1979-1996/7', 1998.

Dobell, Rodney, 'Environmental Degradation and the Religion of the Market', in Harold Coward (ed), *Population, Consumption, and the Environment*, State University of New York Press, Albany, NY, 1995.

Dower, Nigel, 'World Poverty' in Peter Singer (ed), *Blackwell Companions to Philosophy: A Companion to Ethics*, Blackwell's, Oxford, 1990.

Duchrow, Ulrich, *Alternatives to Global Capitalism: Drawn from Biblical History, Designed for Political Action*, International Books with Kairos Europa, Utrecht, The Netherlands, 1998.

Duchrow, Ulrich, Martin Conway, Bob Goudzwaard & AnnCatherin Jarl, *Next Steps towards a Comprehensive Jubilee: An Invitation to Churches and Ecumenical Groups in Western Europe*, World Council of Churches/World Alliance of Reformed Churches/Kairos Europa, Heidelberg, April 2001.

Dupuis, Jacques, SJ, *Toward a Christian Theology of Religious Pluralism*, Orbis Books, Maryknoll, NY, 1997.

Economist, The, London (weekly).

— 'The Puzzling Failure of Economics', 23rd August 1997.

Elfstrom, Gerard, *Moral Issues and Multinational Corporations*, Macmillan, London and St Martins Press, New York, 1991.

Ellacurai, I. & John Sabrino, *Mystericum Liberationis: Fundamental Concepts of Liberation Theology*, Orbis Press, Maryknoll, NY, 1993.

Fisher, Mary Pat, *Living Religions*, I.B. Tauris, London, 1997.

Flannery, Austin, OP (ed), *The Basic Sixteen Documents, Vatican Council II, Constitutions, Decrees, Declarations*, Costello Publishing Company, Northport, NY, April 1996.

Gaffney, Mason & Fred Harrison, *The Corruption of Economics*, Shepheard-Walwyn, London, 1994.

Gaudium et Spes (The Church in the Modern World), Pastoral Constitution of the Second Vatican Council, Catholic Truth Society, London, 1965.

George, Henry, *Progress and Poverty*, 1879, reprinted by Robert Schalkenbach Foundation, New York, 1971.

George, Susan, *How the Other Half Dies*, Penguin Books, New York, 1976.

George de Mille, Agnes, *Who Was Henry George?*, Robert Schalkenbach Foundation, New York, 1979.

Griffiths, Brian, *Morality and the Market Place: Christian Alternatives to Capitalism and Socialism*, Hodder & Stoughton, London, 1982.

Guardian, The, London (daily).

Hick, John & Paul F. Knitter (eds), *The Myth of Christian Uniqueness: Toward a Pluralistic Theology of Religions*, Orbis Books, Maryknoll, NY, 1987.

Howarth, Catherine *et al*, 'Monitoring Poverty and Social Exclusion: Labour's Inheritance' in *Joseph Rowntree Foundation*, December 1998.

Hudson, Michael, G.J. Miller & Kris Feder, *A Philosophy for a Fair Society*, Shepheard-Walwyn in association with Centre for Incentive Taxation Ltd, London, 1994.

Hutton, Will, 'Titanic greed of the telecom giants', in *The Observer*, 22nd April 2001.

Hutton, Will & Anthony Giddens, *On the Edge: Living with Global Capitalism*, Jonathon Cape, London, 2000.

Imbach, J., *Three Faces of Jesus: How Jews, Christians and Muslims see Him*, Templegate Publishers, Springfield, Ill, 1992.

Klein, Naomi, *No Logo*, HarperCollins, London, 2001.

Knitter, Paul, F., *No Other Name? A Critical Survey of Christian Attitudes toward World Religions*, Orbis Books, Maryknoll, NY, 1985.

— *One Earth, Many Religions: Multifaith Dialogue and Global Responsibility*, Orbis Books, Maryknoll, NY, 1995.

Kung, Hans, 'The World Religions in God's Plan of Salvation', in J. Neuner (ed), *Christian Revelation and World Religions*, Burns & Oates, London, 1967.

— *Global Responsibility: In Search of a New World Ethics*, SCM Press, London, 1991.

Kung, Hans & Karl-Joseph Kuschel (eds), *A Global Ethics: The Declaration of the Parliament of the World's Religions*, SCM Press, London, 1993.

Kung, Hans *et al*, *Christianity and World Religions: Paths of Dialogue with Islam, Hinduism, and Buddhism*, Orbis Books, Maryknoll, NY, 1993.

Kuschel, Karl-Josef, *Abraham: A Symbol of Hope for Jews, Christians and Muslims*, SCM Press, London, 1995.

Loewenthal, Kate, M., *The Psychology of Religion*, One World, Oxford, 2000.

Loy, David R., 'The Religion of the Market', in Harold Coward & Daniel Maguire (eds), *Visions of a New Earth: Religious Perspectives on Population, Consumption and Ecology*, State University of New York Press, Albany, NY, 2000.

Maguire, Daniel, 'Catholicism and Modernity', in *Horizons*, 13.2, 1986.

Mater et Magistra (Mother and Teacher), encyclical letter of Pope John XXIII, Catholic Truth Society, London, 1961.

McOustra, Christopher, *Love in the Economy: Social Doctrine of the Church for the Individual in the Economy*, St Paul Publications, Slough, UK, 1961.

Mofid, Kamran, *Development Planning in Iran: From Monarchy to Islamic Republic*, Middle East and North African (MENAS) Press, Wisbech, UK, 1987.

— *The Economic Consequences of the Gulf War*, Routledge, London, 1990.

Moltmann, Jürgen, *God for a Secular Society: The Public Relevance of Theology*, SCM Press, London, 1999.

Munera, Alberto, SJ, 'New Theology on Population, Ecology, and Over-Consumption from the Catholic Perspective', in Harold Coward & Daniel Maguire (eds), *Vision of a New Earth: Religious Perspectives on Population, Consumption and Ecology*, State University of New York, Albany, NY, 2000.

Neuner, J., *Christian Revelation and World Religions*, Burns & Oates, London, 1967.

New Jerusalem Bible, The, Darton, Longman & Todd, London, 1985.

New Statesman, London (weekly).

Niebuhr, Reinhold, *Moral Man and Immoral Society*, Scribners, New York, 1932.

Novo Millenio Inuente (*At the Start of the New Millennium*), Apostolic Letter of John Paul II, Vatican, 6th January 2001.

Noyes, Richard (ed), *Now the Synthesis: Capitalism, Socialism and the New Social Contract*, Holmes & Meier, New York, 1991.

Observer, The, London (weekly).

Ormerod, Paul, *The Death of Economics*, Faber & Faber, London, 1994.

Pacem In Terris (*Peace Throughout the World*), encyclical letter of Pope John XXIII, Catholic Truth Society, London, 1963.

Polanyi, Karl, *The Great Transformation*, Beacon Press, Boston, 1957.

Potter, George Ann, *Deeper than Debt: Economic Globalisation and the Poor*, The Latin Bureau, London, 2000.

Quadragesimo Anno (*The Social Order*), encyclical letter of Pope Pius XI, Catholic Truth Society, London, 1931.

Rerum Novarum (*The Condition of the Working Classes*), encyclical letter of Pope Leo XIII, 1891, Catholic Truth Society, London.

Richards, David, 'Missing Links in the New Economics', *Land and Liberty*, March-April 1987.

Schumacher, E.F., *Small is Beautiful: Economics as if People Mattered*, Bland & Briggs, London, 1973.

— *A Guide for the Perplexed*, Jonathan Cape, London, 1977.

Sen, Amartya, *On Ethics and Economics*, Basil Blackwell, Oxford, 1998.

Singer, Peter (ed), *Blackwell Companion to Philosophy: A Companion to Ethics*, Blackwells, Oxford, 1990.

Smart, Ninian, *Dimensions of the Sacred: An Anatomy of the World's Beliefs*, HarperCollins, London, 1996.

Sollicitudo Rei Socialis (*Social Concern*), encyclical letter of Pope John Paul II, Catholic Truth Society, London, 1987.

Sutherland, Kathryn (ed), *An Inquiry Into the Nature and Causes of the Wealth of Nations*, Oxford University Press, Oxford, revised edition 1998.

Tablet, The, London (weekly).

Tawney, R.H., *The Acquisitive Society*, G. Bell & Sons, London, 1921.

— *Religion and the Rise of Capitalism*, John Murray, London, 1926.

— *Equality*, George Allen & Unwin, London, 1931.

Watkins, Kevin, *Globalisation and Liberalisation: Implications for Poverty, Distribution and Inequality*, UNDP, New York, 1997.

Weber, Max, *The Protestant Ethic and the Spirit of Capitalism*, George Allen & Unwin, London, 1930.

Westminster Interfaith Newsletter, London (monthly).

Whaling, Frank, *Christian Theology and World Religions: A Global Approach*, Marshall Pickering, London, 1986.

Wright, Anthony, *R.H. Tawney*, Manchester University Press, Manchester, 1987.

Young, John, 'Was Henry George Right?', in *Social Justice Review*, September/October 1994.

— *The Natural Economy*, Shepheard-Walwyn, London, 1996.

Index

ALSO FROM SHEPHEARD-WALWYN

Progress and Poverty

**An inquiry into the cause of industrial depressions
and the increase of want with the increase of wealth
... The Remedy**

Henry George

The important social issues raised in this classic of economic literature remain unresolved to this day. George's non-violent solution to poverty has been all but forgotten, although it had widespread support around the world and was endorsed by Churchill and four British Prime Ministers during the 20th century.

Full Edition   ISBN 0 91131 279 X   £24.95 hb
Full Edition   ISBN 0 91131 258 7   £14.95 pb
Abridged Edition   ISBN 0 91131 210 2   £9.95pb

A Philosophy for a Fair Society

Michael Hudson PhD, G.J. Miller MD FRCP, Kris Feder PhD

'Decades of welfare have not dented the inequality of health'
Morning Star

Dr Miller, a fellow of the Royal College of Physicians, argues that welfare capitalism 'has become a social system to which we need to attach a Health Hazard warning'. Using health rather than economic statistics, he shows that the failure of the system to redistribute wealth more equitably has allowed the gap between rich and poor to widen and this disparity is reflected in the lower health and life expectancy of the poor.

Michael Hudson provides a historical survey of the economic conditions leading to social exclusion and the collapse of ancient societies and compares them with conditions in the world today.

Kris Feder restates the philosophy of Henry George, pointing out its relevance to modern conditions.

176pp   ISBN 0 85683 161 1   £22.50 hb · ISBN 0 85683 159 X   £12.95 pb

ALSO FROM SHEPHEARD-WALWYN

The Natural Economy

John Young

'A true grasp of how the economy should be constituted shows it to be a thing of harmony and beauty, all its parts cooperating for the common good, and its inbuilt laws distributing benefits equitably.'
John Young

The author argues that economics is fundamentally an ethical science for it is about an order that is natural to humanity. The implementation of a natural economic order will bring justice; its neglect will bring injustice.

'In its quiet and exact way it is more radically revolutionary than the works of Marx. It is more radical, because it goes more surely to the root of economics. It is also revolutionary, but far from advocating violence, the book begins its revolution by engendering understanding of what is wrong.' **AD 2000**

'The treatment brings out that aspect which is most important to the understanding of matters economic, namely, that it signifies an abundance of goods or wealth for all. This is in stark contrast to the miserable modern vision of scarcity as the guiding principle of all economic thinking.'
Catholic Weekly

160pp   ISBN 0 85683 166 2   £10.95 pb

Christianity and Social Order

Archbishop William Temple

'William Temple was foremost among the leaders of the nation, temporal and spiritual, in posing challenging, radical questions about the nature of our society and its economic basis at a time of world recession, massive unemployment and social despair.'
Edward Heath

The enduring appeal of Temple is that he looks to principle for guidance, writing that 'the art of government in fact is the art of so ordering life that self-interest prompts what justice demands.'

'The link between when [it] first appeared in 1942 and its current publication is the permanent instability of the capitalist economic system and the strains it imposes on living a life worthy of human dignity.' **Labour Monthly**

128pp   ISBN 0 85683 025 9   £5.95 pb